Quick and Easy Menus on A Dime

by Jill Cooper

Cover by: Amy Bleser

Visit us on the Web!
www.LivingOnADime.com
E-mail
editor@livingonadime.com

Table of Contents

Quick and Easy Menus On A Dime

All the recipes in this book can be made with 30 minutes or less preparation time in the kitchen. Some recipes have longer cooking times, like in a crock-pot, or need to be refrigerated but we include them because they are so fast to prepare and easy to get done.

Time Saving Tips

I have found that most meals can be made with about 30 minutes or less preparation time under these conditions:

Keep your kitchen clean.

No one wants to do dishes, then cook and then do dishes again. Clean your kitchen after each meal and you will save one step when starting dinner.

Make sure you have all your ingredients.

Try to prepare some things ahead of time.

- Take meat out of freezer, clean veggies and make gelatins or puddings ahead of time. The less you have to prepare later, the quicker you can cook the meal. Keep cleaned veggies and fruits in the fridge. Serve them on a platter on those busy days.

- No veggies cleaned and no time for a salad? Then just cut wedges of lettuce and serve with dressing.

Keep a master list of menus.

- For one month, keep track of what you make for every dinner. Then you have a list for reference so you don't have to spend as much time planning.

- It doesn't always save to plan menus two weeks in advance. Flexibility allows you to take advantage of unexpected good deals and to adapt if you need to use leftovers. Instead, try planning one or two days in advance.

- Make a habit of planning the next day's dinner after the evening meal's dishes are cleaned. It usually only takes five to ten minutes.

Have family members help:

- There is no reason why the kids can't help with the cleaning, including dishes and other chores, so that you have time to prepare meals.

- Have everyone remove his or her own dirty place setting from the table and put away four or five additional items. The table will be cleared quickly using this method and you won't have to do it all yourself.

- Wash your dishes right away. If you don't let the dishes sit, the food will not get stuck on them. This will save you a lot of time and you won't have to clean the kitchen during the crazy time before the next meal.

- Save time when unloading the dishwasher and set the table for the next meal.

Make simple meals. One-dish meals can contain your meat, your vegetable and your starch.

Put away containers and clean as you cook.

Things to do the night before:
- Plan your meals.
- Put things in the refrigerator to defrost.
- Pack lunches.
- Set the table for breakfast and prepare breakfast foods. For pancakes, mix dry ingredients the previous night. In the morning, add wet ingredients and cook.

Cook Once, Cook Big:

- Make large batches of beans and store in one or two cup portions.

- Make a large batch of granola and store it in an airtight container. If you use it in lunches or snacks, divide it into single-serving plastic bags or containers.

- Brown a large portion of ground beef and store in one-cup portions. You can also do this with roast, pork and round steak.

- Cut extra ingredients for another meal when using onions, green peppers, and other vegetables.

- Cook double batches of rice or pasta to be used later in the week.

Buy staples in quantity if you use them often.

Your freezer is your friend.

- Make double or triple the amount when you prepare main dishes. Freeze. Label with the name of the dish and cooking instructions. Later, when you are too busy to cook, put it in the crockpot on low or set the timer for the oven to start dinner before you get home.

- Place all pre-made meals in one part of the freezer. That way your husband and kids can easily find the meals when you aren't home.

- Besides keeping the usual container in the freezer to dump leftover veggies into, keep one in there for hamburger. Every time I brown some hamburger, I put three to four tablespoons in my container. At the end of a week or two, I will have a pound of "free" hamburger all ready to use.

- Keep your freezer well stocked. Keep frozen fruits and vegetables on hand. It's handy if you always keep packages of chicken, ham, roast or turkey that you have already cooked in the freezer.

Convenience Items Are Cheaper Than Eating Out.

- Use canned foods on busy days. A canned peach half with a dollop of whipped topping and sprinkled with brown sugar looks yummy even to the pickiest eater.

- Keep your pantry well stocked. Don't forget canned meats, too. You can take almost any kind of canned meat -- tuna, chicken, roast or leftover meat and add it to a white sauce. Serve it over toast and you have an instant main dish.

- Keep things in your pantry like boxes of stuffing mix, boxed taco shells, enchilada sauce, puddings, and Hamburger Helper.

- The next time you are at the grocery store, check out the "instant" or "quick" foods. Then pick out enough of your family's favorites to make two or three very fast and easy meals for emergencies.

Tip

The day before you go to the grocery store, clean out your fridge so you can see what leftovers you have so you can include them in your menus.

How To Plan A Menu

Meat or Main Dish
Starch Side Dish (potatoes, rice and pasta)
Vegetable Side Dish (1 fresh or cooked vegetables)
Salad
Bread or Crackers
Dessert
Drink

Try to have a pleasing balance of color.

Do:	Don't:
Chicken	Chicken
Mashed potatoes	Mashed potatoes
Green beans	Corn on the cob
Sliced strawberries or red Jell-O	Banana

Everything on the don't list is basically the same color. Together, these items fade away and don't have the eye appeal as the first list with it's green and red.

Try to include different types of texture.

Do:	**Don't:**
Sausage gravy on toast	Sausage gravy on toast
Hash browns	Creamed peas
Mixed fruit	Creamed potatoes
Jumbo cookies	Vanilla pudding

Everything on the don't list is creamy, runny or soft. You need some crunchy, crispy, soft and in between textures.

Don't serve like items:
- If you have mixed fruit for a salad don't serve fruit pie for desert.

- If you have milk shakes for a drink, don't serve ice cream for dessert.

The old saying -- "too much of a good thing" or in this case "too much of the same thing" definitely applies here.

Most importantly of all, try not to let these tips overwhelm you and cause you to just give up.

You'll find after a couple of months of using my menus that a lot of these things will become habits. Above all, don't worry!

I've never heard of a family dying because once in a while you didn't have the right color of vegetable or were served all soft foods. These are only guidelines not commandments.

If all else fails, don't make your own menus -- just use ours!

Tip

Write down the menu number on your calendar or day planner. Then you'll know at a glance what you need to get at the grocery store, set out of the fridge to thaw or make the day before.

A Kansas Wife

Three men married wives from different states.

The first man married a woman from Michigan . He told her that she was to do the dishes and house cleaning. It took a couple of days, but on the third day, he came home to see a clean house and dishes washed and put away.

The second man married a woman from Missouri . He gave his wife orders that she was to do all the cleaning, dishes and the cooking. The first day he didn't see any results, but the next day he saw it was better. By the third day, he saw his house was clean, the dishes were done and there was a huge dinner on the table.

The third man married a girl from KANSAS . He ordered her to keep the house cleaned, dishes washed, lawn mowed, laundry washed, and hot meals on the table for every meal.

He said the first day he didn't see anything, the second day he didn't see anything but by the third day, some of the swelling had gone down and he could see a little out of his left eye, and his arm was healed enough that he could fix himself a sandwich and load the dishwasher.

(Since we are from Kansas we just had to put this joke in! Jill and Tawra)

Beef

Best BBQ Brisket

6-8 lbs. brisket
3 Tbsp. liquid smoke
salt, pepper, garlic and onion salt
Worcestershire sauce
BBQ sauce (page 16)

Rub liquid smoke on meat. Sprinkle with salt, pepper, garlic and onion salt. Cover and set overnight in refrigerator. Sprinkle with Worcestershire sauce and bake at 275 degrees for 4-6 hours. When done, cover with barbecue sauce.

Tip

Don't forget to run your sink stoppers, scrub brushes, soap dishes and other things like that through the dish washer to keep them clean and shiny.

Barbecue Sauce

1/2 cup ketchup
2 Tbsp. brown sugar and Worcestershire sauce each
1 Tbsp. cider vinegar
1 dash hot pepper sauce
1 tsp. garlic powder
1/4 tsp. mustard powder
1/4 tsp. salt

In a small saucepan over medium heat, stir everything together. Bring to a simmer, then remove from heat and allow to cool slightly before brushing on your favorite meat.

Tip

Have one leftover night a week, where you serve all your little dabs of everything that's left.

```
┌─────────────────────────────────┐
│        Beef Au Jus              │
│      Boiled Potatoes            │
│         Carrots                 │
│    Cinnamon Roll Pudding        │
└─────────────────────────────────┘
```

Beef Au Jus

1 roast
1 packet onion soup mix or
        onion powder, garlic powder,
        salt and pepper (to taste)
potatoes
carrots
rolls

Slow cook a roast with soup mix or spices, potatoes
and carrots in a slow cooker or in the oven 6-8 hours
at 250 degrees.
Slice the roast and serve on Hoagies or large rolls.
Serve with a small bowl of beef juice from the roast to
dip the sandwiches in the juice.

A delicious way to eat the potatoes is to mash them
on your plate, pour some of the "au jus" on them
along with a dollop of butter or sour cream or both.
(Oh, yum!)

Tip

When roasting potatoes always make extra potatoes
to use in other meals. They can be creamed, fried or
used in potato salad.

Cinnamon Roll Pudding

Save those one or two cinnamon rolls or donuts that dry out or get stale and toss them in the freezer. You will always have them then to make this yummy "comfort food" dessert.

2-4 cinnamon rolls or donuts (about 3 cups)
2 eggs
1 1/2 cups milk
3/4 cup sugar
1 tsp. vanilla
1/4 tsp. salt
1/4 cup margarine or butter, melted
2 Tbsp. honey
caramel ice cream topping

Place torn rolls in a 1 quart greased baking dish. In a bowl, slightly beat eggs. Add milk, sugar, salt and vanilla and mix. Pour over rolls. Combine honey and butter and pour over everything. Bake at 300 degrees for 1 hour or until light brown. Serve with caramel topping. Makes 4-6 servings.

Kid Kitchen Terms

Jelly is a food usually found on bread,
kids and piano keys

```
┌─────────────────────────────────────┐
│        Ketchicola Roast             │
│        Mashed Potatoes              │
│        Garlic Green Beans           │
│        Bread, Butter and Jam        │
│        Coconut Brownies             │
└─────────────────────────────────────┘
```

Ketchicola Roast

We are blessed with many good cooks in our family.
This recipe comes from my mother-in-law, Rosella.

1 (3-3 1/2 lb.) beef chuck roast
1 onion, sliced
1 cup ketchup
1 cup cola soft drink
salt and pepper to taste

Season roast and sear on both sides. Place in a
roasting pan or slow cooker. Cover with onion. Mix
ketchup and cola together; pour over roast. Bake
covered 3 hours in the oven at 325 degrees or until
meat is tender. (Or bake 6-8 hours in slow cooker.)
Add additional cola as needed if the liquid cooks
down.

Garlic Green Beans

2 Tbsp. olive oil
3 tsp. cider vinegar
2 tsp. dried onion
2 garlic cloves, finely chopped
salt and pepper
3 cups frozen green beans, thawed
3 Tbsp. bread crumbs
3 Tbsp. Parmesan cheese, grated
1 Tbsp. margarine, melted

Mix first 5 ingredients. Add beans and coat with mixture. Pour into greased baking dish. Mix bread crumbs, cheese and margarine and sprinkle over bean mixture. Bake uncovered at 350 degrees for about 15 minutes. (It just needs to be heated through.)

Kid Kitchen Terms

DESSERT: The reason for eating a meal.

Coconut Brownies

1/4 cup butter, melted
1/4 cup brown sugar
2 eggs
1 tsp. vanilla
3/4 cup flour
1 tsp. baking powder
1/2 tsp. salt
1/2-3/4 cup nuts

Topping:
1/4 cup butter, melted
1/2 cup brown sugar
1 cup coconut

Mix butter, brown sugar, eggs and vanilla. Add flour, baking powder, salt and nuts. Mix well. Pour into a greased 8x8 pan and bake at 350 degrees for 30 minutes or until done. Mix topping ingredients and spread over baked brownies. Place under the broiler (3 inches from heat) to slightly brown coconut.

Tip

Use a plastic knife to cut brownies. They won't stick to the knife.

Blue Cheese Hamburgers

To make Blue Cheese Hamburgers, just crumble some blue cheese into your hamburger before you make it into patties. It enhances the flavor of the hamburger.

Tip

If you are getting tired of having to carefully form another hamburger patty for the barbecue then here's an easy trick my mom always used to make hers.

Tear some wax paper into squares. I usually tear strips about 6 inches wide stack then together and cut the strips in half. This doesn't have to be perfect. You're just making squares that are just a little bigger than your patties.

Now lay down a wax paper square, set a ball of hamburger on it and top with another piece of wax paper. Take a plate and gently press the ball to the thickness that you would like.

A reader cut out the sides of gallon milk jugs and did the same thing and they are reusable.

Potato Salad

6 potatoes, peeled, cubed and boiled
3 eggs, hard boiled and chopped
2 slices bacon, fried and crumbled
2 carrots, peeled and chopped
1 dill pickle, diced
1 tsp. onion powder or 1/4 onion finely chopped,
        or to taste
1 tsp. garlic powder, or to taste
salt to taste

Mix everything in a large bowl. You can adjust the ingredients to add more or less of something if you want.

Dressing:

1/4 cup Miracle Whip
2 Tbsp. to 1/4 cup sour cream
2-3 Tbsp. ranch dressing

I adjust the amount of dressing ingredients depending on how large my potatoes are. You can mix the dressing ingredients together first if you prefer, but I usually mix them right in with the salad ingredients. If the potato salad seems a little dry, I add a couple tablespoons of milk to make it more moist.

*When making potato salad, add the dressing to the warm potatoes. It will absorb the flavor better and give you a better taste.

Hasty Hamburger and Beans

1 lb. hamburger
1 onion chopped
1 can pork and beans
1/4 cup barbecue sauce
salt and pepper to taste
1 cup shredded cheddar cheese (optional)

Brown hamburger and onion. Add beans, barbecue sauce, salt and pepper and heat through. Top with cheese and warm until melted.

Thoughts From 1959

"When I first started driving, who would have thought gas would someday cost 50 cents a gallon. Guess we'd be better off leaving the car in the garage."

Cucumber Salad

4 medium cucumbers, peeled and diced
1 (6 oz.) container vanilla low-fat yogurt
1 (8 oz.) container reduced-fat sour cream
1/2 cup diced onion
2 cloves garlic, minced
1 Tbsp. dried dill weed
 salt and pepper to taste

Drain cucumbers for a few minutes on paper towels.
In a serving dish, stir together the yogurt, sour cream,
onion, garlic, and dill. Add cucumbers, and gently mix
to coat. Season with salt and pepper. Refrigerate for a
couple of hours before serving for best flavor.

Tip

On days when everyone is eating at a different time,
serve things that keep well. For example, in place of a
cooked vegetable serve a platter of fresh vegetables
or stews and casseroles instead of fried pork chops.

Banana Split Dessert

Crust:
2 cups graham cracker crumbs
1/2 cup butter or margarine, melted

Mix and press into a 9x13 pan.

1st Layer:
2 cups powdered sugar
1 cup butter, softened
1 tsp. vanilla
2 eggs (may use egg substitute)

Mix together and beat for 2 minutes. Then pour over crust.

Topping:
3 bananas, sliced
1 cup strawberries, sliced
12 oz. crushed pineapple, drained
3 cups whipped topping
1 cup nuts, chopped
chocolate sauce and cherries

Spread 1st layer with bananas, strawberries and pineapple. Cover with whipped topping and sprinkle with nuts. Chill for at least 12 hours. Serve with chocolate sauce and cherries.

```
┌─────────────────────────────────┐
│          Taco Pie               │
│           Corn                  │
│         Fruit Cup               │
└─────────────────────────────────┘
```

Taco Pie

This is especially good with crescent rolls, but if you don't have any, you can press canned biscuits into the pan for the crust.

1 can crescent rolls
2 cups corn chips, crushed (divided)
1 pkg. taco seasoning
1 lb. ground beef, browned
1 cup sour cream
4 oz. grated Mexican cheese (or cheddar)

Separate crescent rolls into triangles and press into the bottom of a pie pan. Sprinkle crushed corn chips over crescent roll crust. Mix taco seasoning and hamburger and spread over corn chips. Spread sour cream on next and sprinkle cheese on top. Top with 1 cup of corn chips. Bake at 400 degrees for 15-20 minutes.

Fruit Cup

15 oz. can tropical fruit
1 sliced banana
20 oz. can pineapple
coconut

Mix and chill. Sprinkle with coconut before serving.

Tip

Keep several cans of fruit in the fridge. That way
when you make fruit salads they are always nice and
cold and you don't have to wait to chill them.

Taco Wraps

1/2 lb. hamburger, cooked
2/3 to 3/4 cup sour cream
2 Tbsp. taco seasoning
1 cup cheddar or Mexican mix cheese, grated
1 tomato, finely chopped
3/4-1 cup lettuce, thinly shredded
5-6 flour tortillas

Mix sour cream and taco seasoning. Spread on tortillas. Layer 1-2 tablespoons of the rest of the ingredients on each tortilla and roll up. Serve with salsa.

Thought Of The Day

God gave us zucchini to force us to make new friends.

Orange Salad

6 cups salad greens or spinach
2 medium oranges, peeled and sliced
1/2 cup red onion, coarsely chopped
1/4-1/2 cup blue cheese, crumbled
1/4 cup slivered almonds, toasted

Dressing

1/3 cup vegetable or olive oil
1/4 cup orange juice
1 Tbsp. vinegar
1 clove of garlic, minced
1/4 tsp. salt

Mix dressing. Arrange salad greens on plate. Layer with oranges and sprinkle with onion. Drizzle with dressing then sprinkle with blue cheese and almonds.

Tip

If you hate cooking at home but want to start to save money, then reward yourself you giving yourself a tip for each dinner you make. Place the same amount of tip you would pay if you went out it eat into a jar. At the end of the month use that money for something special like a kitchen appliance to make cooking easier, disposable pans, or something pretty for your kitchen.

Angelic Strawberry Dessert

This is the best summer dessert! Keep 2 or 3 of them made and in the freezer for unexpected or out of town company. It's also a great dessert for a bridal shower, a graduation or a summer party.

1 (1lb.) angel food cake (You can use a larger one --
        the filling just won't be as thick)
1 (8 oz.) package cream cheese, softened
1 can vanilla frosting
1 pint of fresh strawberries, sliced

Mix cream cheese and frosting, Cut cake in thirds horizontally. Spread bottom layer with half of the frosting mixture and then layer with half of the strawberries.

Place the next layer of cake on top of that and spread with the other half of frosting and strawberries. Add top layer of cake. Wrap and freeze.

When you need it, set it out to thaw slightly before cutting.

Tip

For an easy way to clean your microwave just wipe it down after you get done cooking anything that causes it to steam up (like a baked potato).

Mystery Meatballs

meatballs
grape jelly
ketchup

Make your favorite meatball recipe or buy pre-packaged meatballs. Place in a crockpot. Mix equal parts grape jelly and ketchup, enough to cover the meatballs. Cook about 2 hours on low.

This sounds crazy but this is one of our favorite recipes! We also use it on chicken, Yum!

Green and Gold Salad

1/4 cup salad oil
2 tsp. vinegar
salt and pepper to taste
1 can (1 lb.) green beans
1 can (11 oz.) mandarin oranges, drained
1/4 cup onion rings, thinly sliced
1 cup herb seasoned croutons
2-3 cups bite sized pieces of iceberg or romaine lettuce

Mix oil, vinegar and salt and pepper in salad bowl. Add remaining ingredients and toss. Serves 6.

Joe Froggers Cookies

This is a very old recipe which was popular years and years ago in this country. Note that there are no eggs in this recipe. Not everyone owned a chicken and eggs were expensive so for many recipes they improvised when they didn't have an ingredient.

1 cup sugar
1/2 cup shortening
1 cup dark molasses
1/2 cup water
1 1/2 tsp. salt
1 tsp. baking soda
1 1/2 tsp. ground ginger
1/2 tsp. ground cloves
1/2 tsp. nutmeg
1/4 tsp. ground allspice
4 cups flour
sugar

Cream 1 cup sugar and shortening. Add remaining ingredients. Cover and refrigerate at least 3 hours. You can either roll out 1/4 inch thick and cut into 3 inch circles or roll into balls and press flat with a floured glass on a well greased cookie sheet. Sprinkle tops with sugar before baking at 375 degrees for 10-12 minutes or until almost no imprint is left when lightly touched. Cool 2 minutes before removing from cookie sheet.

Cranberry Spinach Salad

1 Tbsp. butter
3/4 cup almonds, blanched and slivered
1 lb. spinach, rinsed and torn into bite-size pieces
1 cup dried cranberries
2 Tbsp. toasted sesame seeds
1 Tbsp. poppy seeds
1/2 cup white sugar
2 tsp. minced onion
1/4 tsp. paprika
1/4 cup white wine vinegar
1/4 cup cider vinegar
1/2 cup vegetable oil

In a medium saucepan, melt butter over medium heat. Cook and stir almonds in butter until lightly toasted. Remove from heat, and let cool.

In a large bowl, combine the spinach with the toasted almonds and cranberries.

In a medium bowl, whisk together the sesame seeds, poppy seeds, sugar, onion, paprika, white wine vinegar, cider vinegar, and vegetable oil. Toss with spinach just before serving.

This is my absolute favorite salad! Every time I serve it people just rave about it! Tawra

34

S'More Bars

8-10 whole graham crackers
1 package brownie mix
2 cups mini marshmallows
1 cup chocolate chips
2/3 cup chopped peanuts

Arrange graham crackers in a 9x13 pan. Mix brownie batter according to directions on package. Pour over graham crackers. Bake at 350 degrees for 25-30 minutes until a toothpick inserted in center comes out clean. Sprinkle with marshmallows, chocolate chips and peanuts. Bake 5 minutes longer until marshmallows are melted, puffy and golden. Cool before cutting.

Thought Of The Day

Charity is baking for the church bazaar; compassion is buying it back.

Pinwheel Pizza Loaf

2 eggs
salt and pepper to taste
3 lbs. ground beef
6 thin slices deli ham
2 cups (8 oz.) mozzarella cheese, shredded
1 jar (14 oz.) pizza sauce

In a bowl slightly beat eggs, salt and pepper. Mix in ground beef. On a piece of wax paper or foil, pat mixture into a 12x10 rectangle. Cover with ham, sprinkle with cheese within a half inch of the edge. Roll up jelly roll style, starting at the short end. Peel foil away as you roll. Seal seams and ends of loaf. Place seam side down on a greased 9x13 pan and top with pizza sauce. Bake uncovered at 350 degrees for 1 1/4 hours until meat is no longer pink. Let set 10 minutes before slicing.

Boston Cream Pie Cupcakes

1 pkg. yellow cake mix
1 cup milk
1 pkg. (4 serving size) vanilla instant pudding
1 1/2 cups whipped topping, thawed, divided
1 cup (about 8 oz.) chocolate chips

Bake cake mix into to cupcakes according to package directions. Cool. Mix milk and pudding with whisk until thickened. Fold in 1/2 cup of the whipped topping into the pudding. With serrated knife, cut cupcakes horizontally in half. Spoon 1 Tbsp. of pudding mix on bottom half and cover with the top of the cupcake. Mix remaining whipped topping and chocolate chips and heat 1 minute in the microwave until chips are melted. Check every 30 seconds and stir. Frost cupcakes with about 1 1/2 tsp. of chocolate mix. Chill for 15 minutes. Store leftovers in fridge.

Tip

When spraying pans with cooking spray or flouring them, hold them over the sink and all the overspray will go in the sink.

Mexican Spaghetti

This recipe has several ingredients but is so easy because it mostly just calls for dumping in cans of things.

1 lb. ground beef, cooked, drained
3/4 cup onion, chopped
1 jar (26 oz.) meatless spaghetti sauce
1 can (15 oz.) black beans, rinsed and drained
1 can (14 1/2 oz.) diced tomatoes
1 cup frozen corn, thawed
1 cup salsa
1 can (4 oz.) chopped green chilies
1 Tbsp. chili powder
salt and pepper to taste
cooked spaghetti - enough for your family

In large saucepan, cook the meat and onion. Drain. Add remaining ingredients, except the spaghetti. Bring to a boil. Reduce heat and simmer uncovered 10-15 minutes. Serve over spaghetti. Serves 10. Freeze or refrigerate leftover sauce.

Marbled Strawberry Cake

1 pkg. white cake mix
1 pkg. (4 serving size) strawberry gelatin
2/3 cup sour cream
2/3 cup powdered sugar
1 tub (8 oz.) whipped topping, thawed
1 1/2 cups sliced strawberries

Mix cake batter according to directions. In a 9 inch cake pan, pour 1/4 of the batter on just one half of the pan. Do the same in a second pan. Mix strawberry gelatin into remaining batter then pour 1/2 of that into the other side of each pan. Take a spoon and carefully marble the two sides together. Don't mix too much. Bake at 350 degrees for 30 minutes.

Mix sour cream and sugar. Fold in whipped topping. Place one cake layer on a serving dish and spread with 1 cup of whipped topping mix. Next, layer 1 cup of the strawberries and top with the remaining cake layer. Frost with the rest of the whipped topping and garnish with the last of the strawberries. Store leftovers in the refrigerator.

Bean 'N' Beef Quesadillas

1 1/2 cups chunky salsa
1/4 cup minced fresh cilantro or
      1 Tbsp. dried
3 Tbsp. lime juice
1 cup canned black beans, rinsed and drained
1/2 cup frozen corn, thawed
2 cups chopped cooked roast beef
2 cups shredded Monterey Jack cheese
8 (10 inch) flour tortillas
1 Tbsp. vegetable oil

In a small bowl, combine the salsa, cilantro and lime
juice. In another bowl, combine the beans, corn and
1/2 cup of the salsa mixture. Set remaining salsa
mixture aside.

Place beef, cheese and bean mixture on half of each
tortilla; fold over. In a large skillet over medium heat,
cook quesadillas in 1 tablespoon oil for 1-2 minutes
on each side or until cheese is melted, using
additional oil as needed. Cut into wedges. Serve with
reserved salsa mixture.

Grandma's Banana Dessert

This very simple dessert was always served at my husband's family dinners. Everyone, young and old alike, loved this old fashioned favorite.

2 (3oz.) pkgs. instant banana pudding
4 cups milk
2-3 bananas
vanilla wafer cookies
1 small container whipped topping
nuts, chopped, optional

Prepare pudding according to the package directions and set aside. Cover the bottom of a 9x13 pan with vanilla wafers. Place a layer of sliced bananas on top of vanilla wafers, then spread with pudding. Top it all with whipped topping and sprinkle with nuts. Chill. Best served the same day.

Tip

Having trouble getting your children to eat their food at dinner time?

Try serving just water for a beverage. A lot of times children fill up on juice, milk or pop before they even get food on their plates. They are not as likely to tank up on liquid if that liquid is water.

Beefy Burgers

1 lb. ground beef
1 egg
1/3 cup bread crumbs
1 can beefy mushroom soup
1 can French fried onions

Mix first 3 ingredients and shape into 4-5 large patties. Brown patties on both sides and then cover in soup. Simmer 20 minutes. Top with French fried onions.

"Cool" Veggie Salad

1 head cauliflower, cut into pieces
1 bunch broccoli, cut into pieces
10 oz. frozen peas
1/4 to 1/2 cup onion, chopped

Dressing
1 cup sour cream
1 cup salad dressing (like Miracle whip)
1 pkg. Hidden Valley Ranch dressing mix

Mix ingredients. Pour over veggies and chill overnight. This will keep well in the fridge for several days.

Butterscotch Pudding Parfaits

1 box butterscotch pudding
whipped Cream or whipped Topping
nuts (optional)

Make pudding according to the directions on the box.
Layer in parfait glasses with whipped topping.
Sprinkle nuts on top if desired.

Kid Kitchen Terms

SODA POP: Shake 'N Spray.

TABLE LEG: Percussion instrument.

EVAPORATE: Magic trick performed by children when
it comes time to clear the table or wash dishes.

Pizza Bake

1 pkg. macaroni and cheese
1 lb. ground beef
1 medium onion, sliced
1 small green pepper, sliced (optional)
1 cup (4 oz.) cheddar cheese, grated
1 (14 oz.) can pizza sauce
1 (3-4 oz.) pkg. pepperoni slices
1 cup (4 oz.) mozzarella cheese

Cook macaroni, drain and add only the cheese packet. Pour into a 9x13 pan or baking dish and sprinkle with cheddar cheese. In a pan, cook beef, onion and pepper. Drain and spread over macaroni. Pour pizza sauce on top. Add pepperoni and mozzarella cheese. Bake uncovered at 350 degrees for 20 to 25 minutes, just until heated through.

Strawberries over Cream

This is a nice light dessert. It is not too sweet.

1 envelope (1 Tbsp.) unflavored gelatin*
3/4 cup cold water
1 cup sour cream
1 small container whipped topping
      with 1 tsp. vanilla stirred in
2 pints strawberries, sliced

Pour water into a sauce pan, sprinkle with gelatin and dissolve over low heat. Stir in sour cream. Remove from burner and cool. When slightly cool, add whipped topping. Pour into a mold, pan or bowl and chill. Serve topped with sliced strawberries.

*Don't be afraid of unflavored gelatin. You can find it at the store by the Jell-O and it is just as easy to use.

Tip

Don't forget to add some vanilla to the whipped topping for more body and flavor.

Pork

```
┌─────────────────────────────────────┐
│      So Delicious Pork Chops         │
│      Country Fried Potatoes          │
│           Caesar Salad               │
│           Fresh Bread                │
│          Butter and Jam              │
│       Instant Peach Cobbler          │
└─────────────────────────────────────┘
```

So Delicious Pork Chops

6-8 pork chops
1 cup ketchup
1 cup Coke

Brown pork chops and place in a greased baking dish. Mix ketchup and coke and pour over chops. Cover and bake at 375 degrees for 30-45 minutes.

Thoughts From 1959

"Did you hear the post office is thinking about charging a dime just to mail a letter?"

Instant Peach Cobbler

Filling

1/4 cup butter, melted
1 can peach pie filling (or any other fruit filling)

In a greased casserole dish, mix butter and pie filling.

Topping

1 can refrigerator biscuits, cut in fourths
1/4 cup butter, melted
1/2 cup sugar
1 tsp. cinnamon

Mix sugar and cinnamon. Dip biscuits into melted butter and then into the sugar mixture. Place them on top of fruit filling. Bake at 400 degrees for about 15-20 minutes until biscuits are brown.

Thought Of The Day

A sure way to get rich quick - count your blessings

Tropical Coleslaw

1 can (20 oz.) pineapple tidbits,
    drained reserve 2 Tbsp.
1 Tbsp. lemon juice
1 medium banana, sliced
3 cups cabbage, shredded
1 can (11oz.) mandarin oranges, drained
1 cup mini marshmallows
1 cup flaked coconut
1 cup walnuts, chopped
1 cup raisins
1/2 tsp. salt
1 carton (8 oz.) pineapple yogurt

Mix reserved pineapple juice, lemon juice and
banana. Add remaining ingredients, adding yogurt last
to toss and coat. Cover and chill until ready to serve.

Garlic Broccoli

2 Tbsp. olive or vegetable oil
1 Tbsp. lemon juice
1 clove of garlic, minced or crushed
salt and pepper to taste
1 lb. broccoli, cooked

Mix first 4 ingredients. Toss with cooked broccoli.
If you mix the "dressing" early and let it set it helps the
garlic flavor to blend into the oil.

You may add cherry tomatoes for garnish before
serving.

Kids!

Little Johnny watched, fascinated, as his mother
smoothed cold cream on her face. 'Why do you do
that, mommy?' he asked. 'To make myself beautiful,'
said his mother, who then began removing the cream
with a tissue. 'What's the matter?' asked Little Johnny.
'Giving up?'

Nutty Ham Pitas
Chips
Sliced Tomatoes/Cucumbers
Chocolate Coconut Bars

Nutty Ham Pitas

1 cup ham, cooked and diced
1 hard boiled egg, chopped
1/2 cup cheddar cheese, grated
1/2 cup pecans, chopped
2/3 cup sour cream
2 Tbsp. green onions, chopped
4 pita bread, halved

Mix all but bread. Spoon into bread. Makes 4 servings

Kids!

Little Johnny's at it again..... A new teacher was trying to make use of her psychology courses. She started her class by saying, 'Everyone who thinks they're stupid, stand up!' After a few seconds, Little Johnny stood up. The teacher said, 'Do you think you're stupid, Little Johnny?' 'No, ma'am, but I hate to see you standing there all by yourself!'

Chocolate Coconut Bars

1 tube (8 oz.) refrigerated crescent rolls
1 pkg. (8 oz.) cream cheese, softened
1/3 cup powdered sugar
1 egg
3/4 cup flaked coconut
1 cup chocolate chips
1/4 cup nuts

Unroll and press rolls into a 9x13 pan, pressing perforations together and press dough slightly up the sides of the pan. Cream cream cheese, sugar and egg until smooth. Stir in coconut and spread on crust. Bake at 375 degrees for 10-15 minutes until it is set. Sprinkle immediately with chips and let stand 5 minutes. Spread melted chips. Sprinkle with nuts. Cool before cutting.

No Mess Dinner

1 pork chop, about 4 oz.
1 medium potato, sliced
1 large carrot, sliced
1/4 cup frozen peas
1 Tbsp. onion soup mix

Lay pork chop on a double thick piece of heavy duty foil, about 18 x14 inches. Layer with potato, carrot, and peas and sprinkle with soup mix. Seal well. Place on grill and cook covered over medium heat for about 30 minutes or until meat juices run clear. Turn occasionally.

Chocolate Peanut Butter Pizza

1 (17 1/2 oz.) pkg. peanut butter cookie mix*
12 oz. cream cheese, softened
1 3/4 cups milk
1 (3.9 oz.) pkg. instant chocolate pudding
1 (8 oz.) container whipped topping
1/4 cup chocolate or peanut butter chips

Prepare cookie dough according to the directions and press into a 12 inch pizza pan. Bake at 375 degrees for 15 minutes. Whip cream cheese in a bowl until smooth and spread over cooled crust. In the same bowl, mix milk and pudding for 2 minutes. Spread over cream cheese. Refrigerate until set, about 20 minutes.

Top with whipped topping and sprinkle with chips. Chill for 1-2 hours.

*Note: You can use your own homemade cookie dough if you want. If there is extra dough left over, just bake it into cookies while you are baking the above or freeze to use later. Experiment with different cookie dough. For example, use sugar cookie or chocolate chip dough in place of peanut butter.

Baked Pork Chops and Potatoes

6 pork chops
salt and pepper
1/3 cup onions, chopped
vegetable oil
4 cups potatoes, thickly sliced
1 can cream of mushroom soup
1 1/4 cups milk

Pour a couple of teaspoons of vegetable oil in a pan;
add onions and sauté. Add pork chops that have been
seasoned with salt and pepper; brown on both sides.

Place potatoes in a 2 quart greased baking dish and
arrange browned chops on top. Add the soup and milk
to the cooked onions in the skillet. Stir and heat. Pour
on top of chops and potatoes.

Bake covered for 30 minutes at 350 degrees. Uncover
and bake 30-40 more minutes. Serves 6.

```
┌─────────────────────────────────────┐
│        BLT Sandwiches                │
│   (bacon, lettuce and tomato)        │
│      German Baked Beans              │
│    Raspberry Rhapsody Salad          │
└─────────────────────────────────────┘
```

Raspberry Rhapsody Salad

1 (6 oz.) pkg. raspberry Jell-O
2 cups boiling water
2 cups raspberry sherbet
1/2 to 1 cup frozen or fresh raspberries

Dissolve Jell-O in boiling water. Add sherbet and stir until melted. Add raspberries and chill until set.

You can change the Jell-O to orange and use orange sherbet and mandarin oranges or strawberry Jell-O with strawberry sherbet and strawberries.

Tip

If you have an extra package of the cheese that comes in a box of macaroni and cheese dinner, sprinkle some of it onto a piece of buttered corn.

German Baked Beans

1/2 lb. hamburger
1/2 cup chopped onions
1 (12 oz.) can pork and beans
1 cup applesauce
1 Tbsp. mustard
1/2 cup brown sugar
1 cup catsup
salt and pepper to taste

Fry hamburger with onions until brown. Add it and everything else into a large casserole dish. Bake at 350 degrees for 30 minutes. In the summer, I would put this in a crockpot. If you don't have a crockpot then simmer on the stove, stirring occasionally.

Tip

Put some chili powder in cheddar cheese biscuits for extra flavor.

Fried Ham

4 thick ham slices
1 Tbsp. margarine or butter

Melt margarine or butter in a pan on medium heat.
Add ham slices. Fry on one side for 3-4 minutes or
until brown. Flip and fry on other side until brown.
Serve warm. Makes 4 servings.

Tip

Wash potatoes and then rub the outside with bacon
grease. Place in a crockpot and cook on high for 3-4
hours or low for 8 hours. You will have the yummiest
and easiest baked potatoes ever!

Strawberry Dessert

This is probably one of my favorite desserts, partly because it is not too rich. It is an especially good dessert to keep made in the freezer for when unexpected company comes by. I like to use it for parties, and other get-togethers because I can make it a week ahead of time!

Crust:
1 cup flour
1/4 cup brown sugar
1/2 cup nuts
1/2 cup butter, softened

Mix and slightly press or crumble into a 9x13 pan. Bake at 350 degrees for 20 minutes. Stir occasionally while baking to make crumbly. When cooled, remove 1/3 of it and save to sprinkle on top of the dessert. Evenly spread out the remaining portion in the pan.

Topping:
2 egg whites (may use pasteurized)
2/3 cup sugar
1 (10 oz.) pkg. frozen strawberries
2 Tbsp. lemon juice (must use)
1 small container whipped topping

Place first 4 ingredients in a large bowl. Beat on high speed for 10 minutes or until it forms stiff peaks. Be sure to use a large mixing bowl because this really increases in volume. Fold in whipped topping and spread over crust, Sprinkle with the 1/3 cup of crumbs you saved back. Freeze 3-6 hours or overnight.

Marinated Pork Chops

3/4 cup vegetable oil
1/3 cup soy sauce
1/4 cup vinegar
2 Tbsp. Worcestershire sauce
1 Tbsp. lemon juice
1 Tbsp. prepared mustard
1 tsp. salt
1 tsp. pepper
1 tsp. dried parsley flakes
1 garlic clove, minced
6 (1 inch thick) pork chops

Combine the first 10 ingredients in a large resealable plastic bag or shallow glass container; add pork and turn to coat. Seal bag or cover container; refrigerate 3 hours or overnight. Drain and discard marinade. Grill, covered, over medium coals, turning occasionally, for 20-25 minutes or until juices run clear.

Fruit Salad

1 (11 oz.) can mandarin oranges, drained
1 (8 oz.) can pineapple chunks, drained
1 medium ripe banana, sliced
1/2 cup halved seedless grapes
3 Tbsp. mayonnaise
3 Tbsp. sour cream
1 Tbsp. honey
1/4 cup chopped walnuts
1/4 cup flaked coconut

In a bowl, combine the fruit. In another bowl, combine the mayonnaise, sour cream and honey. Pour over fruit and toss to coat. Cover and refrigerate. Just before serving, stir in walnuts and coconut if desired.

Tip

Use your vegetable peeler to peel fruits too like pears, apples or kiwis.

```
┌─────────────────────────────────────┐
│         Ham Sandwiches               │
│      Chips and Barbecue Dip          │
│         Sliced Tomatoes              │
│         Corn on the Cob              │
│          Orange Floats               │
└─────────────────────────────────────┘
```

Barbecue Dip

Here's another great dip for when unexpected company drops in or you need something quick.

1 cup sour cream
1/2 to 3/4 cup barbecue sauce

Mix ingredients. I usually don't measure anything in this recipe. I just start adding the barbecue sauce to the sour cream until it tastes good. It's really yummy with plain old potato chips.

Tip

Cook corn on the cob like you normally do but for a different twist sprinkle with Parmesan cheese and garlic powder after you have buttered it.

Orange Floats

Vanilla ice cream
Orange soda

Place one scoop of ice cream in a tall glass and pour a small amount of orange soda on it. Add another scoop and more soda. Repeat this until your glass is full. Top with whipped topping and/or an orange slice.

Tip

Mix and match all the menus and recipes in this cookbook. You will be able to make hundreds of combinations!

Sausage Balls

1 lb. sausage
3 cups baking mix
8 oz. cheddar cheese, grated

Partially cook sausage and drain. Mix with baking mix and cheese. Form into 1 1/2 to 2 inch balls. Bake at 375 degrees for 20 minutes.

Sliced Potatoes

4 medium potatoes, peeled and sliced
2 Tbsp. margarine
1/2 to 1 cups cheddar cheese, grated

Place the first 2 ingredients in greased microwave proof dish. Cook on high for 4 minutes or until tender. Sprinkle with cheese and cook until cheese is melted. Serves 4.

Hot Ham and Cheese Sandwiches

4 slices ham
4 slices Swiss or your favorite cheese
Spicy Sandwich Sauce (optional)
8 slices bread
margarine or butter

Heat a skillet on medium heat. Spread margarine or butter on one side of each slice of bread. Cook until brown on each side.

Spicy Sandwich Sauce

1/4 cup butter, softened
2 Tbsp. prepared horseradish mustard
2 Tbsp. chopped onions
1 tsp. poppy seeds
1 tsp. dill seed

Combine butter, mustard, onions, poppy seeds and dill seed. Spread insides of buns with this mixture. Place a slice of cheese and a slice of ham inside each bun.

Cottage Cheese Potato Salad

1 cup cottage cheese
3/4 cup mayonnaise
2 tsp. salt (to taste)
1/4 tsp. pepper, to taste
3 hard boiled eggs, chopped
4 large potatoes, cooked and cubed
1 cup celery, diced
1/2 cup radishes, sliced
1/2 cup green bell pepper, diced
1/2 cup green onions, diced
2 Tbsp. sliced black olives

Mix first 4 ingredients in large bowl. Add remaining ingredients and mix well.

Tip

To make this go very quickly, slice and dice the veggies and hard boil the eggs the day before. A food chopper makes this go super fast!

```
┌─────────────────────────────────┐
│        Apple Pork Chops          │
│          Green Beans             │
│      Bowl of Baby Carrots        │
│       Marshmallow Bars           │
└─────────────────────────────────┘
```

Apple Pork Chops

6 pork chops
1 Tbsp. oil
1 package of stuffing mix, crushed
1 can (21 oz.) apple pie filling

Brown chops in oil. Prepare stuffing according to package directions. Spread pie filling into a greased 9x13 pan. Top with pork chops then spread with stuffing. Cover and bake at 350 degrees for 35 minutes. Uncover and bake 10 minutes longer.

Green Beans

For extra flavor in your green beans, brown 3 tablespoons of butter (Heat in saucepan until it starts to brown or caramelize. Watch carefully!) Then add drained beans and toss. Also you can heat your beans with a little bacon grease and onion powder.

Marshmallow Bars

1 (18 oz.) devil's food cake mix
1/4 cup butter or margarine, melted
1/4 cup water
1 egg
3 cup mini marshmallows
1 cup plain M & M's
1/2 cup chopped peanuts

Mix cake mix, butter, water, egg. Pat into a greased 9x13 pan. Bake at 375 degrees for 20-25 minutes until a toothpick inserted in the center comes out clean. Sprinkle with remaining ingredients and bake 2-3 minutes longer until marshmallows begin to melt. Cool before cutting.

Tip

If you don't have time to frost a cake just sprinkle chocolate chips, white chocolate chips, peanut butter chips or peppermint chips on your cake.

Easy Fruit Salad

1 can apple pie filling, cut slices in pieces
1 can (15 oz.) fruit cocktail, drained
1 cup mini marshmallows
1/2 cup chopped nuts

Mix and serve.

Barb's Cherry Dessert

2 cans cherry pie filling
2 Jiffy white cake mixes
1 stick butter, melted

Spread the pie filling on a cookie sheet with a 1 inch side. Sprinkle cake mix on top. Drizzle melted butter over the top. Bake at 350 degrees until browned.

Chicken

Mexican Summer Squash

4 yellow summer squash
4 ears corn
3 ripe tomatoes
1/4 cup butter
1 small onion, chopped
salt and pepper (to taste)

Wash squash and cut into small pieces. Cut corn from the cob. Skin tomato and cut into cubes. (The skin comes off easily if the tomatoes are first dipped in boiling water for one minute.)

Heat butter in a saucepan. Stir in onion and cook until limp but not brown. Add squash, corn, tomatoes, salt and pepper.

Cover and cook over a low heat for 30-40 minutes, stirring occasionally. If desired, serve over cooked rice. Serves 4.

Lemon Fluff

This is such a light and not overly sweet dessert for summer:

1 3/4 cups milk
2 (3 oz.) pkgs. vanilla instant pudding
1 (12 oz.) can frozen lemonade concentrate (thawed)
1 (8 oz.) tub whipped topping
pie crust (optional)

Mix milk and pudding in bowl with whisk for 30 seconds. Add lemonade and whisk 30 more seconds. Fold in whipped topping. Chill 4 hours. You can use this with or without a pie crust.

Thought Of The Day

Hospitality is making your guests feel at home, even though you wish they were.

```
┌─────────────────────────────────┐
│      Barbecue Chicken            │
│      Apple Bacon Salad           │
│      Country Fried Potatoes      │
│      Frozen Fruit Cocktail       │
└─────────────────────────────────┘
```

Apple and Bacon Salad

If you are tired of the usual tossed salad, here's a new twist on it that has lots of flavor and color.

1/2 head Boston lettuce
1/2 head leaf lettuce
2 carrots, peeled and diced
1 red apple, diced
1/2 cup cheddar cheese, shredded
4 slices bacon, cooked and crumbled*

Vinaigrette:

1/2 cup olive oil
2 Tbsp. red wine vinegar
1/2 tsp. dry mustard
1/4 tsp. oregano
pinch of salt, pepper and sugar

Whisk the vinaigrette ingredients together in a salad bowl. Then add all of the salad ingredients on top of it and toss.

*To save time and make this salad easier, fry extra bacon when you cook breakfast in the morning and save it to use for the salad. You could also use bacon bits.

Country Fried Potatoes

6 potatoes, peeled and sliced
2-3 Tbsp. bacon grease (You can use margarine but the flavor isn't quite the same.)

Melt grease in a frying pan. Add potatoes and cook over medium high heat. When golden brown flip to the other side and cook until side is brown and potatoes are tender. Salt and pepper to taste.

Frozen Fruit Cocktail

8 oz. cream cheese, softened
1 (16 oz.) can fruit cocktail

Whisk or beat cream cheese until smooth. Drain fruit. Mix into cream cheese and pour into a loaf pan (or any freezer proof container that is about that size). Freeze. Thaw slightly before you are ready to serve. Slice like you would slice bread. Sometimes a warm knife makes it easier.

This can be served with a dollop of whipped cream for dessert or on a lettuce leaf for a salad. You can also use other kinds of canned fruit but the fruit cocktail tastes really good frozen like this.

Mrs. B's Chicken
New Red Potatoes, Boiled
Fruit Salad
Corn
Dinner Rolls
Cherry Delight

Mrs. B's Chicken

6-8 pieces chicken, floured and placed in a 9x13 pan
2 cups hot water
1 tsp. (or 2 cubes) chicken bouillon
1 bay leaf
onion salt to taste
mushrooms
1/4 tsp. thyme
3/4 cup heavy cream

Dissolve bouillon in water and add the bay leaf, onion salt and mushrooms. Pour over chicken. Cover and bake at 350 degrees for 1 hour and 45 minutes. Add thyme and cream and finish baking uncovered for 15 minutes.

Cherry Delight

1 can (12-16 oz.) dark sweet pitted cherries
1 can (about 16 oz.) crushed pineapple
1 (8 oz.) pkg. cream cheese, softened
1 pkg. marshmallows
1 small container of whipped topping
 pecans, chopped (optional)

Drain cherry and pineapple juices into a medium
sauce pan. Dissolve cream cheese in juices over low
heat. Add marshmallows and dissolve. Cool
completely and fold in cherries, pineapple and
whipped topping. Pour into a serving dish or bowl and
chill for a few hours to set.

Tip

Line your vegetable drawer in your fridge with a paper
towel. It helps to absorb the liquid from you veggies
and then when you clean out the drawer next just
scoop up the paper towel, crumbs and all, and toss.

```
┌─────────────────────────────────────┐
│        Chicken Pitas                 │
│        Potato Salad                  │
│   Fresh Veggies Of Any Sort          │
│        Baked Beans                   │
│        Watermelon                    │
└─────────────────────────────────────┘
```

Chicken Pitas

1-2 cups chicken, cooked
1/2 cup cucumbers, largely diced
1 carrot, sliced
3-4 radishes, sliced
1/4 cup black olives, sliced
4-8 oz. mozzarella cheese, grated
1/3 cup Italian salad dressing
5 pita breads, halved

In a bowl, combine everything and toss with dressing. Line pitas with lettuce and fill with chicken mix.

Tip

If you need to cut boneless, skinless chicken, it cuts easier if it is slightly frozen.

Saucy Chicken

4-6 pieces of chicken
1 can of cream of chicken soup

Place chicken in pan that is lined with foil or greased well. Spread with soup and cover. Bake at 250 degrees for 1 1/2 to 2 hours or 350 degrees for 1 hour. Serve chicken and the sauce that the soup made on top of rice.

Sunshine Dessert

1 pkg. (3 oz.) lemon Jell-O
2 cups boiling water
1 pint lemon sherbet, softened
1 Tbsp. grated lemon peel
whipped topping

Dissolve Jell-O in water. Stir in sherbet and lemon peel. Pour into dessert glasses, cover and chill. Refrigerate overnight. Garnish with whipped topping.

```
Chicken Salad Sandwiches
Tater Tots with melted cheese
Fresh Seasonal Veggies
Frozen Peach Dessert
```

Chicken Salad Sandwiches

For a different twist serve these on hamburger or hot dog buns. If you are counting the calories, serve on a lettuce leaf.

chicken, cooked and cubed
celery, chopped
walnuts, peanuts or cashews, chopped
salad dressing (Miracle Whip)

Mix and serve.

Here are some other things to add to your chicken salad if you have them on hand:

crumbled bacon
cucumbers
pineapple
chopped green olives
chopped hard-boiled eggs

water chestnuts
green onions
almonds
grapes

Frozen Peach Dessert

1 can peach halves
strawberries, frozen or fresh
whipped topping

Place a strawberry in the center of each peach half. Top with whipped topping and freeze. Thaw 15-20 minutes before serving. This makes a great after school snack for those first few hot days back to school.

Tip

When making gelatin salads with canned fruit, don't throw away the reserved juice. Use part of it in place of the water you are supposed to use.

Roasted Veggie Platter

1 bell pepper, cut in chunks
1 red onion, cut in wedges
1 yellow squash, cut into 1/2 inch slices
1/2 lb. whole fresh mushrooms
1/4 lb. fresh green beans, trimmed
1/4 cup Italian dressing
1/4 tsp. dried basil
1/4 tsp. dried thyme
1/4 tsp. dried rosemary, crushed

Place veggies on a greased 15x10x1 pan. Drizzle
with dressing and sprinkle with herbs.

Bake uncovered at 450 degrees for 15-20 minutes or
until vegetables are tender.

Crunchy Ice Cream Dessert

Make this ahead of time for a quick dessert for company or for the family at the end of a busy day.

2 cups crushed Rice Chex cereal
2/3 cup packed brown sugar
1/2 cup chopped peanuts
1/2 cup flaked coconut
1/2 cup butter or margarine, melted
1/2 gallon vanilla ice cream
      (buy the rectangular shaped package)

Combine first 5 ingredients. Press half into a 13x9 ungreased pan. Cut ice cream into 3/4 inch slices and arrange over crust. Top with remaining crumb mix, pressing down lightly. Cover and freeze until ready to serve.

Tip

Want a good soup recipe?
Just let your ice cream melt. Ha Ha!

```
┌─────────────────────────────────────┐
│        Chicken Nuggets              │
│     Cheesy Rice with Peas           │
│         Tossed Salad                │
│   Watermelon wedges or sliced       │
│            apples                   │
└─────────────────────────────────────┘
```

Chicken Nuggets

1/2 cup seasoned bread crumbs
2 Tbsp. grated Parmesan cheese
1 egg white
1 lb. boneless, skinless chicken breast cut into cubes

Pour crumbs and cheese in a resealable plastic bag. Beat egg white in a bowl. Dip chicken in egg white, then shake in with crumbs mix. Place on a 15 x 10 x 1 inch baking pan sprayed with cooking spray. Bake at 400 degrees for 12-15 minutes until chicken is no longer pink. Turn once.

Cheesy Rice with Peas

2 1/4 cups cooked rice
1 package (10 oz.) frozen peas, thawed
1 jar (6 oz.) mushrooms, drained
6 oz. Velveeta, cubed

Mix everything in a greased 1 1/2 quart baking dish. Cover and bake at 350 degrees for 20 minutes, until heated through.

Chicken Croissants

2 cups chicken, cooked and cubed
1/4 cup celery, diced
1/4 cup golden raisins
1/4 cup dried cranberries
1/4 cup sliced almonds
3/4 cup mayonnaise or salad dressing
2 Tbsp. chopped red onion
salt and pepper to taste
4 croissants

Mix everything but croissants. Spoon 1/2 cup of the mixture into each croissant.

Banana Cake

1 package (18 oz.) yellow cake mix
1 package (3.4 oz.) instant banana pudding mix
1/4 cup vegetable oil
4 eggs
1 cup water
1 1/2 cups (about 2 medium) mashed ripe bananas
3/4 cup chopped walnuts

Beat first 5 ingredients for 2 minutes. Add bananas and mix well. Fold in nuts. Pour in a greased 9x13 pan.

Bake at 350 degrees for 50-55 minutes or until a toothpick inserted in the center comes out clean. You may dust with powdered sugar or frost with vanilla or cream cheese frosting.

Tip

If you have guests frequently popping in to your home, keep a tray with all the elements for hot drinks like tea bags, hot chocolate mix, hot cider creamers, sugar, instant coffee.

Then, when the guests show up unexpectedly, it's just a matter of putting the kettle on for hot water so you have more time with your guests.

```
┌─────────────────────────────────────┐
│          Picante Chicken             │
│           Brown Rice                 │
│          Spinach Salad               │
│   No Bake Peanut Butter Cookies      │
└─────────────────────────────────────┘
```

Picante Chicken

You might want to double this recipe and use it for leftovers to shred for taco salad, burritos or fajitas.

4 chicken breast halves, skinless (or 1lb. chicken)
1 (16 oz.) jar picante sauce
3 Tbsp. brown sugar
1 Tbsp. prepared mustard
optional - a little chili powder and garlic powder for extra seasoning

Place chicken in shallow 2 quart baking dish. Combine the remaining ingredients and pour on the chicken. Bake covered for 1 hour at 350 degrees or 400 degrees for 30-35 minutes or double and place frozen in a crockpot for 4 hours on low.

No Bake Peanut Butter Cookies

1 cup sugar
1 cup corn syrup
1 jar (12 oz.) crunchy peanut butter
5 cup rice crispy cereal

Melt sugar and syrup. Add peanut butter and mix. Add cereal. Form into 1 inch balls and place on wax paper, cool.

```
+--------------------------------+
|      Chicken Stir Fry          |
|          Rice                  |
|      Sliced Tomatoes           |
|      Poppy's Biscuits          |
|      Brownie Cake              |
+--------------------------------+
```

Aunt Kathleen's Chicken Stir Fry

1 1/2 to 2 cups chicken, thinly sliced
1 Tbsp. oil
1 pkg. stir fry vegetables
1/4 tsp. salt
1/4 tsp. black pepper
1/2 to 1 tsp. leaf thyme
2 Tbsp. butter
1/4 cup water

Fry chicken in oil in a large frying pan until cooked through. Add remaining ingredients to the pan and heat thoroughly. Serve over rice.

Poppy's Biscuits

These biscuits are so yummy! If you have ever had Popeye's biscuits you will know what I mean. These are a really close match.

Don't be afraid of these because they are made from scratch. They are really very simple, with only 4 ingredients. I have known many inexperienced cooks who had great success with biscuits. Try them. I think you'll like them!

4 cups baking mix (Bisquick)
3/4 cup club soda
8 oz. sour cream
1 stick butter

Melt butter in 9x13 pan. Combine remaining ingredients. Place dough on lightly floured surface and knead lightly. Pat or roll out to 1/2 inch thickness. Cut with a biscuit cutter or glass. Place in the pan and turn over once, making sure they are well coated in butter. Bake at 400 degrees until brown (15-20 minutes). If you want, you can drizzle a little extra butter on top.

Brownie Cake

1 pkg. brownie mix
1 cup (8 oz.) sour cream
1 (6 oz.) bag chocolate chips
1/2 cup walnuts, chopped
chocolate frosting

Mix brownie mix as directed. Add everything else but frosting. Pour into a 9x13 greased pan and bake at 350 degrees for 30-35 minutes. Cool and frost with frosting.

Thought Of The Day

Sitting still and wishing
Makes no person great:
The good Lord sends the fishing,
But you must dig the bait!
(from The Art of Homemaking
by Daryl Hoole)

Chef Salad
Assorted Crackers
Royal Fruit Cup
Angel Food Delight

Royal Fruit Cup

1 can (20 oz.) pineapple chunks, drained
1 can (15 1/4 oz.) sliced peaches, drained
1 cup strawberries, sliced
1 cup cantaloupe and/or honeydew,
    cut into bite sized pieces
1 cup cream soda, chilled
2 Tbsp. sugar
1 tsp. cinnamon
1 banana, sliced

Combine first 5 ingredients. Mix sugar and cinnamon. Stir into fruit. Cover and refrigerate 2-4 hours. Add banana just before serving.

Thought Of The Day

We pray in microwave time but the answer usually comes slow cooked.

Angel Food Delight

1 angel food cake, cubed
1 can pie filling (cherry, peach or blueberry)
1 small pkg. instant vanilla pudding
1 1/2 cups milk
1 cup sour cream
whipped topping

Place half of the angel food cake cubes in a pan or dish (about a 9 inch square size). Top with pie filling. Place remaining angel food cake on top.

In a separate bowl, combine pudding, milk and sour cream, beating well. Pour over cake. Chill for 5 hours or more. Serve topped with whipped topping.

Tip

Keep a couple of angel food cakes in your freezer for when you need a quick dessert. You can top them with any fresh fruit you have on hand. Add a dollop of whipped topping and you are good to go. In a pinch you can even spread with some fruit jam, and/or pudding and whipped cream.

```
+------------------------------------------+
|           Roast Chicken                  |
|        Spicy Sweet Potatoes              |
|           Green Beans                    |
|    Fresh Carrot And Celery Sticks        |
|        Mint Brownie Cake                 |
+------------------------------------------+
```

Juicy Roasted Chicken

1 (3 pound) whole chicken, giblets removed
salt and black pepper to taste
1 Tbsp. onion powder, or to taste
1 Tbsp. garlic powder to taste (optional)
1/2 cup margarine, divided
1 stalk celery, leaves removed, cut into 3 pieces

Preheat oven to 350 degrees. Place chicken in a roasting pan, and season inside and out with salt, pepper and onion powder. Place 3 tablespoons margarine in the chicken cavity. Arrange dollops of the remaining margarine around the chicken's exterior. Place celery in the chicken cavity.

Bake uncovered 1 hour and 15 minutes to a minimum internal temperature of 180 degrees. Baste with melted margarine and drippings. Cover with foil, and allow to rest about 30 minutes before serving.

This is how we make our turkey for Thanksgiving, except we cook it at 275 degrees for 8-10 hours.

Spicy Sweet Potatoes

3 large sweet potatoes, peeled and
       cut into 1 inch cubes*
2 Tbsp. olive or canola oil
2 Tbsp. brown sugar
1 tsp. chili powder
1/2 tsp salt
1/4 tsp. cayenne pepper

In a resealable plastic bag or container, toss potatoes and oil. Add remaining ingredients and toss again. Pour everything into an 11x7 baking dish. Bake uncovered at 400 degrees for 40-45 minutes or until tender.

*You could use a couple of cans of sweet potatoes instead of fresh sweet potatoes and that would cut down your prep time and baking time. Then, it would take about 30-35 minutes or until tender.

Mint Brownie Cake

1 box brownie mix
2 pkgs. (8 oz.) cream cheese, softened
1 1/2 cups sugar
1 tsp. peppermint extract
2 (8 oz.) containers whipped topping, thawed
green food coloring (optional)
1/2 cup chocolate chips

Bake brownie mix according to the box directions in a well greased pan. Beat cream cheese, sugar, and peppermint extract together. Fold in whipped topping and food coloring. Spread over brownies.

Cover and chill for at least an hour. Just before serving, melt chocolate chips and drizzle on top. Serve with whipped topping or ice cream.

You could halve this recipe and bake in two 9x9 pans. Save one pan of brownies for regular brownies and then make half of the topping ingredients for the other pan.

Fish

Not Your Grandma's Tuna Salad

1 head of lettuce
1 pint cherry tomatoes, halved
4 hard cooked eggs, cut into wedges
4 oz. Swiss cheese, julienned
2 cans (6 oz.) tuna, drained
1/2 cup sliced red onion
balsamic or Miracle Whip dressing

Arrange lettuce leaves on a plate. Top with tomatoes, eggs, cheese, tuna and onion. Drizzle with Balsamic dressing or mix equal parts Miracle Whip and milk to pour on it.

Fruit Slush Cups

4 cups water
1-1 1/2 cups sugar
3/4 cup orange juice concentrate
3/4 cup lemonade concentrate
3 medium firm bananas, sliced
2 (15 oz.) cans tropical fruit salad
  (could use fruit cocktail instead), drained

Cook water, sugar and orange juice and lemonade concentrates until sugar is dissolved. Add fruit and pour into a shallow 3 quart freezer container. Cover and freeze overnight.

Remove from the freezer one hour before serving. You can serve it this way, scooping out what you need or you could pour it into individual paper cups and freeze.

```
┌─────────────────────────────────────┐
│        Tomato/Basil Fish            │
│         Garlic Bread                │
│            Rice                     │
│      Cauliflower/Olive Salad        │
└─────────────────────────────────────┘
```

Tomato/Basil Fish

1/3 cup onion
1 garlic clove, minced
2 tsp. olive oil
1 (14 oz.) can Italian diced tomatoes, drained (may
        use 1 seeded fresh tomato)
1 1/2 tsp. fresh basil, finely chopped
1 lb. fish fillets
4 oz. feta cheese, crumbled

Saute onion and clove in oil. Add tomatoes and basil.
Turn down heat and simmer uncovered for 5 minutes.
Meanwhile, broil fish 5 inches from heat for 5 minutes.
Top fish with tomato mix, sprinkle with cheese and
broil for 5-7 minutes more until fish are flaky.

Cauliflower/Olive Salad

1 head cauliflower
2 green onions
1 cup black olives
ranch dressing

Cut up ingredients. Toss with dressing.

Simple Baked Fish and Chips

2 large potatoes
1/4 cup Italian dressing
1 packet Shake and Bake
      extra crispy seasoned, divided*
1 lb. fish fillets
1/4 cup Miracle Whip dressing

Cut each potato lengthwise into 8 wedges. Toss and coat with Italian dressing. Add 1/4 cup Shake and Bake. Toss and coat. Place on a baking sheet that has been sprayed with cooking spray. Bake 20 minutes.

While those are baking, sprinkle the rest of the Shake and Bake on a plate. Spread the top of each fillet with Miracle Whip and press into the Shake and Bake. While still on the plate, spread the other side with Miracle Whip, flip and press other side with Shake and Bake. Place on a broiler pan, add the potatoes and bake the fillets and the potatoes for 15 minutes or until the fish are flaky and the potatoes are tender. Makes 4 servings.

*For those of you who have our Dining on a Dime cookbook, check out our recipe for homemade Shake and Bake.

Cherry Marshmallow Dessert

1 1/2 cups (24 squares) graham crackers, crumbled
1/3 cup butter or margarine, melted
1 can (21 oz.) cherry or blueberry pie filling
3 cups mini marshmallows
1 (8 oz.) container whipped topping, thawed

In a 9 inch square pan, mix butter and graham
crackers. Then press into the pan to make the crust.
Bake at 350 degrees for 10-12 minutes. Cool, then
top with pie filling. Mix marshmallows with whipped
topping and spread on top. Garnish with graham
cracker crumbs if you want.

Thought Of The Day

A mother's patience is like a tube of toothpaste - it is
never quite all gone.

```
┌─────────────────────────────────────┐
│         Feta Tomato Fish            │
│          Veggie Pasta               │
│       Orange Cream Dessert          │
└─────────────────────────────────────┘
```

Feta Tomato Fish

This is a very light and refreshing way to make fish. For an even fresher taste, try using fresh tomatoes in place of canned tomatoes if you have them.

1/3 cup chopped onion
1 garlic clove, minced
2 tsp. olive oil
1 (14.5 oz.) can Italian diced tomatoes, drained
1 1/2 tsp. minced fresh basil
1 lb. walleye, bass or other whitefish fillets
4 oz. crumbled feta cheese

In a saucepan, saute onion and garlic in oil until tender. Add tomatoes and basil. Bring to a boil. Reduce heat. Simmer uncovered for 5 minutes. Meanwhile, broil the fish 4-6 inches from the heat for 5-6 minutes. Top each fillet with the tomato mixture and cheese. Broil 5-7 minutes longer or until fish flakes easily with a fork.

Veggie Pasta

Cook your favorite spaghetti noodles or pasta. Toss with olive oil, add a few chopped green onions, a can of sweet peas or leftover broccoli. Season to taste with salt and pepper.

Orange Creme Dessert

2 cups orange sherbet,softened
1 pkg. (8 oz.) cream cheese, softened
1 can (14 oz.) sweetened condensed milk
1/2 cup orange juice
1 tub (8 oz.) whipped topping

Line a 9x5 loaf pan with foil. Spread sherbet on the bottom. Freeze 10 minutes.

Beat cream cheese, milk and juice. Fold in whipped topping. Pour over sherbet.

Freeze 3 hours. Remove from mold by inverting the pan onto a plate. You could garnish with mandarin oranges if you like.

Thought Of The Day

Advice is like cooking. You should try it first before you feed it to others

```
┌─────────────────────────────────────┐
│        Parmesan Baked Fish          │
│            Wild Rice                │
│           Green Beans               │
│           French Bread              │
│       Colorful Fruit Compote        │
└─────────────────────────────────────┘
```

Parmesan Baked Fish

1/4 cup mayonnaise
2 Tbsp. grated Parmesan cheese
1/8 tsp. cayenne pepper
4 fillets (1lb.) fish
2 tsp. lemon juice
10 butter crackers (Ritz), crushed

Preheat oven to 400 degrees. Mix mayonnaise,
cheese and pepper. Place fish on a lined shallow pan.
Drizzle the fish with lemon juice, spread with
mayonnaise mix and sprinkle with crackers. Bake
12-15 minutes or until fish flakes with a fork.

Colorful Fruit Compote

2 medium peaches, sliced
1 cup fresh or frozen blueberries
1 cup fresh strawberries, halved
1 cup seedless grapes, red or green
2 kiwi, peeled, sliced
3 Tbsp. apple jelly
4 tsp. water
Vanilla yogurt and sliced almonds, optional

Mix fruits in bowl. Heat jelly and water in the microwave about 45 seconds or until melted. Stir and drizzle over fruit. Top with yogurt and almonds.

Pecan Fish

1/2 cup cornmeal
1 tsp. salt
1/4 tsp. ground black pepper
1 tsp. cajun seasoning (optional)
1/2 tsp. red pepper (optional)
dash cayenne pepper (optional)
1 1/4 lbs. catfish or any other fish filets
3 Tbsp. vegetable oil
1/2 cup pecans, finely crushed

Preheat oven to 400 degrees. Mix the cornmeal and all of the spices.* Dip the catfish in the cornmeal mixture, coating well. Place the catfish on a flat, greased baking sheet. Pour the oil over the fish.

Bake for 15 minutes or until fish flakes easily when tested with a fork. Sprinkle with pecans toward the end of the cooking period. Garnish with lemon wedges.

* To save on clean-up, you can mix the seasonings on a piece of wax paper.

Vegetable Rice Medley

1 Tbsp. vegetable oil
1 medium onion, chopped
1 medium carrot, chopped
1 stalk celery, chopped
1/2 cup red peppers, chopped
1 can (14 1/2 oz.) chicken broth
1 1/2 cups Minute white rice, uncooked
1 cup frozen peas

Heat oil in a saucepan. Add onion, carrot, celery and peppers and cook 5 minutes or until tender. Add broth and bring to a boil. Add rice and peas. Cover and simmer 5 minutes. Remove from heat and let stand 5 minutes before serving. Makes 4 servings.

Easy Chocolate Dipped Peanut Butter Cookies

1 cup creamy peanut butter
1/2 cup sugar
1 egg
1/3 cup chocolate chips, melted
1/2 cup finely chopped peanuts

Preheat oven to 325 degrees. Mix peanut butter, sugar and egg. Chill 30 minutes. Roll into 15-18 balls. Place 2 inches apart on an ungreased cookie sheet. Flatten each ball with a criss cross pattern, using a fork. Bake 18-20 minutes. Cool. Dip each end of the cookie into melted chocolate then into peanuts.

Meatless
and
Miscellaneous

Fried Egg Sandwich

2 tsp. butter
4 eggs
4 slices processed American cheese
8 slices toasted white bread
salt and pepper to taste
 2 Tbsp. mayonnaise
 2 Tbsp. ketchup

In a large skillet, melt butter over medium high heat. Crack eggs in a pan and cook to desired firmness. Just before eggs are cooked, place a slice of cheese over each egg.

After cheese has melted, place each egg on a toasted slice of bread. Season eggs with salt and pepper. Spread mayonnaise and ketchup on remaining slices of bread and cover eggs with bread to make 4 sandwiches. Serve warm.

Fruit Dip

1 cup brown sugar
1/2 cup butter
1 cup sour cream
3 tsp. vanilla extract

In a saucepan, over medium heat, stir the butter and brown sugar together. Remove from heat when the butter has melted.

In a medium mixing bowl, whip together the butter mixture, sour cream and vanilla. Serve warm or allow the dip to chill and thicken in the refrigerator for 2 hours.

Thoughts From 1959

"I'll tell you one thing, if things keep going the way they are, it's going to be impossible to buy a week's groceries for $20."

Slow Cooked Corn Chowder

2 1/2 cups milk
1 (14 oz.) can creamed corn
1 (10 oz.) can cream of mushroom soup
1 3/4 cups frozen corn
2 cups frozen hash browns (or diced potatoes)
1 cup of ham or turkey or sausage chunks
1 onion, chopped
2 Tbsp. butter or margarine
salt and pepper to taste

Mix everything in a crockpot. Cook on low for 6 hours.
You can mix the night before, store it in the fridge and
start cooking in the morning.

Candy Bar Truffle

1 chocolate cake mix (baked as directed)
2 (3 oz.) boxes instant chocolate pudding (Mix as
     directed on the box right before using)
16 oz. container whipped topping
1 cup crushed candy bars - your choice,
     Heath, Hershey's, Butterfinger or
     flavored chips (peanut butter, butterscotch,etc.)

Cut cake into 2 inch cubes. Layer in a bowl*.

Layer, in this order: 1/2 cake, pudding, whipped
topping, candy bars. Repeat.

*This looks nice in a glass bowl.

Tip

Save any leftover Halloween or Easter candy for this
recipe. (Yeah right... as if there is ever any left!)

Mexican Chef Salad

This recipe is so perfect for a hot summer day!

1 head lettuce, chopped
tomatoes, peppers and onions, chopped
1 can Ranch Style beans
        (could substitute cooked hamburger for beans)
1 pkg. corn chips
Catalina Dressing
cheddar cheese, grated

Mix lettuce, tomatoes, peppers and onions. Top with Ranch Style beans and place corn chips around edges. Top with Catalina Dressing and cheddar cheese.

Quick Salsa

1/2 jalapeno pepper, seeded and chopped
1 large tomato, chopped
1 Tbsp. fresh cilantro
1 clove garlic, minced
1 small onion, chopped

Mix and chill for 20 minutes before serving.

Hoagie Sandwiches

assorted breads and rolls
assorted cold cuts
assorted cheeses
tomatoes
lettuce
pickles
olives

Spread mayonnaise and mustard on bread as desired. Layer cold cuts and cheeses. Top with lettuce, tomatoes, pickles and olives. Put a toothpick in the center of each half and slice crosswise before serving.

Thoughts From 1959

"I don't know about you, but if they raise the price of coffee to 15 cents, I'll just have to drink mine at home.

One Dish Vegetarian Meal

It is amazing how something so quick and easy can be soooo good!

1 (16 oz.) package penne pasta, cooked
4 cloves garlic, minced
3/4 cup olive oil
1 large head fresh broccoli, blanched
1 (6 oz.) can sliced black olives
seasonings*

Cook garlic in olive oil in a skillet over medium heat, being careful not to allow the garlic to burn.

Place the cooked broccoli, pasta, and black olives into a large bowl.

To serve, pour garlic oil over pasta and vegetables. Serve warm.

*You can add extra seasonings and/or your favorite cheeses to this dish. Try things like lemon pepper, Italian seasoning, red pepper flakes, onions, Parmesan cheese and feta cheese.

Apple Yogurt Muffins

2 cups flour
1/2 cup sugar
3 tsp. baking powder
1/2 tsp. salt
1/4 tsp. ground cinnamon
1 carton (6 oz.) vanilla yogurt
2 Tbsp. milk
1 egg
1/4 cup vegetable oil
1 small tart apple, peeled and chopped

Topping:

2 Tbsp. flour
2 Tbsp. sugar
1/2 tsp ground cinnamon
1 Tbsp. cold butter or margarine (the stick kind)

Combine the 5 dry ingredients. Combine the 4 wet ingredients and add to dry. Stir just until moistened. Fold in apples. Fill greased or paper lined muffin cups 2/3 full.

For topping, mix all ingredients, cutting in butter until mix is crumbly. Sprinkle on muffin batter.

Bake at 400 degrees for 20-24 minutes or until a toothpick comes out clean.

Chocolate Cheese Bars

This is an easy recipe to double.

1 tube (18 oz.) refrigerated chocolate chip
      cookie dough*
1 pkg. (8 oz.) cream cheese, softened
1/2 cup sugar
1 egg

Press half of the cookie dough into a greased 8x8 pan for crust. Beat cream cheese, sugar and egg until smooth. Spread over crust. Crumble the remaining dough over the top.

Bake at 350 degrees for 35-40 minutes or until a toothpick inserted comes out clean. Refrigerate leftovers.

* I keep 2 cups of my own chocolate chip cookie dough in the freezer to use for these.

Chili Stuffed Potatoes

4 large potatoes, baked
1 can (15 oz.) chili
1/2 cup cheddar or Mexican blend cheese, grated
1 cup tomatoes, diced
1/4 cup sour cream
1/4 cup cilantro, optional

Warm chili in the microwave. Cut an X in the top of a hot baked potato and fluff the insides with fork. Top with chili, cheese, tomato, sour cream and cilantro.

You could add lettuce or hamburger to this recipe if you like or use low fat sour cream and cheese or vegetarian chili.

Peanut Butter Cream Pie

3/4 cup hot fudge sauce, divided
1 graham cracker crust*
1/2 cup peanut butter
1 1/4 cup milk
2 pkgs. (3 oz.) vanilla instant pudding
1 (8oz.) tub whipped topping, thawed and divided

Pour 1/2 cup of hot fudge over the bottom of the pie crust. Place in the freezer for 10 minutes. Mix peanut butter and milk with a whisk, blending well.

Add dry pudding mixes. Beat 2 minutes, blending well. Fold in half of the whipped topping and spread in the crust. Top with the rest of the whipped topping. Chill for 2 hours and drizzle the rest of the hot fudge on top just before serving.

*This would taste great in a chocolate pie crust!

Grilled Apple Swiss Cheese Sandwich

This is best made with wheat bread and Granny Smith apples.

2 slices whole wheat bread
1 1/2 teaspoons olive oil or margarine
1/2 Granny Smith apple
      peeled, cored and thinly sliced
1/3 cup shredded Swiss cheese

Lightly brush one side of each slice of bread with the olive oil. Place one slice of bread, olive oil side down into the skillet and arrange the apple slices evenly over the top. Sprinkle Swiss cheese over the apple, top with the remaining slice of bread, olive oil-side up.

Cook until the bread is golden brown, then flip the sandwich and cook until golden brown and the cheese has melted.

Bacon Tomato Spinach Salad

1/2 lb. bacon, diced and cooked-
       reserve 2 Tbsp. of drippings
1/3 cup Catalina salad dressing
1/2 tsp. mustard
1/4 tsp. salt
1/8 tsp. pepper
2 medium tomatoes, cut in wedges
8 cups fresh spinach
1/2 cup crumbled blue or feta cheese

Add dressing, mustard, salt and pepper to bacon
drippings and heat through on low heat. Mix
remaining ingredients in a bowl and drizzle with warm
dressing mix. Toss.

Thought For The Day

I think if I have a good breakfast, I could go without
food for the rest of the day. I think that until about
lunchtime.

```
┌─────────────────────────────────────┐
│        Hot Jam Sandwiches            │
│     Piece of Fruit or Fruit Cup      │
│           Cheese Egg                 │
│           Coffee/Tea                 │
└─────────────────────────────────────┘
```

Menu: Breakfast for Singles

Hot Jam Sandwiches

1/4 cup butter or margarine
1/4 cup flaked coconut
1/2 cup apricot jam
1/2 tsp. ground cinnamon
12 slices raisin bread

Mix butter and coconut in a bowl. Stir in jam and cinnamon. Spread between slices of bread. Grill on a greased skillet until golden brown on both sides.

Tip

Mix the first 4 ingredients and keep them in your fridge. On those mornings when you don't have time to grill sandwiches, just spread it on raisin toast, a muffin, English muffin, bagel or biscuit and take it with you. This is great on a winter day as an after school snack or with coffee and tea with a friend.

Cheese Egg

This is a simple recipe for teaching kids who are beginning to cook. You could also put it on an English muffin with a sausage patty or some bacon.

1 tsp. butter or bacon grease
1 egg
2 Tbsp. milk
1 slice cheese

Melt butter in a small skillet over medium heat. Whisk together egg and milk in a small bowl. Pour into a skillet. Cook until bubbles appear, then flip over. Cover with cheese. Cook until cheese is melted.

Tip

Save bacon grease in a jar in the refrigerator. Then when you just need a teaspoon or two you'll have it handy.

Quesadilla Jalapeno Spread

This would be great spread on burgers, tacos or chicken sandwiches. It tastes like Taco Bell quesadillas.

1/4 cup mayonnaise
2 tsp. diced canned jalapeno peppers
2 tsp. juice from canned jalapeno peppers
1/2 tsp. ground cumin
3/4 tsp. sugar
1/2 tsp. paprika
1/8 tsp. cayenne pepper
1/8 tsp. garlic powder
dash salt
flour tortillas

Place everything but the tortillas in a blender. Blend until smooth and jalapeno is completely pureed, about 1 minute. Season to taste with salt, as needed. Spread on a tortilla and fold in half.

Lightly oil a frying pan and brown on one side, then on the other. You can add other things to the tortillas before you fry them like chicken, hamburger or cheese.

Quick Elephant Ears

1 1/2 cups sugar
2 teaspoons ground cinnamon
oil for frying
10 (7 inch) flour tortillas

Combine sugar and cinnamon in a shallow bowl or
large plate. Set aside. Heat a half inch of oil in a
skillet. Place one tortilla at a time in the skillet. Cook
for 5 seconds; turn and cook 10 seconds longer or
until browned. Place in sugar mixture and turn to coat.
Serve immediately.

Tip

If you don't have flour tortillas, try using canned
biscuits. Flatten them and bake as directed.

```
┌─────────────────────────────────────┐
│      Swiss Cheese Potato Soup         │
│             Crackers                  │
│           Veggie Platter              │
│     Bea's Pumpkin Apple Cobbler       │
└─────────────────────────────────────┘
```

Swiss Cheese Potato Soup

4 potatoes, peeled and diced
1 small carrot, finely chopped
1/2 stalk celery, finely chopped
1 small onion, minced
1 1/2 cups vegetable broth
1 tsp. salt
2 1/2 cups milk
3 Tbsp. butter, melted
3 Tbsp. all-purpose flour
1 Tbsp. dried parsley
1/2 tsp. ground black pepper
1 cup shredded Swiss cheese

In a large saucepan, bring potatoes, carrots, celery,
onion, vegetable broth and salt to a boil. Reduce heat.
Cover and simmer until potatoes are just tender. Do
not drain. Stir in milk.

In a small bowl, blend butter, flour, parsley, and
pepper. Whisk into potato mixture. Cook and stir over
medium heat until thickened and bubbly.

Remove from heat. Add cheese and stir until cheese
is almost melted. Let soup stand for 5 minutes.

Bea's Pumpkin Apple Cobbler

8 small apples or an equal amount of bigger ones
        (peeled, cored and sliced)
3/4 cup apple butter
1/2 box (14 ounce) pumpkin bread mix
4 Tbsp. butter or margarine
Cool Whip

In a bowl, stir together apples and apple butter. Spread in a greased 8 or 9 inch pan. Pour pumpkin bread mix into another bowl and cut in butter or margarine. Sprinkle over apple mixture. Bake at 350 degrees for about 45 minutes or until apples are tender. Top with cool whip.

```
┌─────────────────────────────────┐
│      Mini Breakfast Pizzas       │
│         Creamy Grapes            │
│         Hash Browns              │
│         Orange Juice             │
└─────────────────────────────────┘
```

There is nothing wrong with having breakfast for dinner. Here is a menu that would work for either.

Mini Breakfast Pizzas

8-10 eggs, scrambled
10 frozen dinner rolls, thawed*
10 bacon strips, cooked and crumbled*
2 cups cheddar cheese

Roll frozen dinner rolls into 5 inch circles and place on greased baking sheet. Top each one with eggs, bacon and cheese. Bake at 350 degrees for 15 minutes until cheese is melted.

*You could use leftover diced ham or cooked ground sausage. If you want to make your own dinner rolls check out our recipe in Dining on a Dime for Ninety Minute rolls.

Creamy Grapes

1 lb. seedless grapes
1 cup (8 oz.) sour cream
1/4 cup brown sugar

Remove grapes from stems and place in dessert cups. Mix sour cream and sugar. Refrigerate until serving time. Spoon over grapes. Serves 6

Red Beans and Rice Burrito
Cool Gelatin Salad
Corn
Sliced Tomatoes

Red Beans and Rice Burrito

You could use leftover beans and rice for this and add chopped tomatoes, green onions, or a different type of cheese for variety.

1 (8 oz.) box red beans & rice mix (such as Zatarains)
8 (10 inch) tortillas
1/2 cup sour cream
1 cup shredded Cheddar cheese
4 tsp. Creole seasoning

Cook rice as instructed on package. Place tortillas in microwave and heat on High for 10 seconds.

Spoon 1/4 cup rice and beans down the center of each tortilla. Top each with 1 tablespoon sour cream, 2 tablespoons Cheddar cheese, and 1/2 teaspoon Creole seasoning. Fold edges over to enclose filling.

Cool Gelatin Salad

1 (3 oz.) pkg. lemon gelatin
1 (3 oz.) pkg. lime gelatin
1 cup boiling water
1 can sweetened condensed milk
8 oz. large curd cottage cheese
1 cup mayonnaise
1 (15 oz.) can crushed pineapple in heavy syrup

Dissolve gelatin in boiling water. Pour in remaining ingredients and chill.

Tip

Try exchanging meals with another family.
Set up a system where you cook double the amount and take half over to another family. Later, they cook double and bring it to you. This means there is one less night that you have to cook and it brings variety to your menu.

Holiday Menus

Valentine's Day

Chicken Marinara
Spinach and Strawberry Salad
French Bread with garlic butter
Aunt Donnie's Cherry Dessert

Chicken Marinara

2 boneless, skinless chicken breasts
1 (3 oz.) pkg. cream cheese, softened
1 envelope garlic-herb soup mix, divided
1/3 cup water
1 Tbsp. olive oil
3 oz. pasta(uncooked) - your choice of
        spaghetti noodles or angel hair
1 1/2 cups spaghetti sauce, warmed
1/2 cup mozzarella cheese, shredded

Carefully slice a pocket in each chicken breast, being sure to leave it attached along the edge. Mix cream cheese and 2 teaspoons of soup mix. Stuff into pockets and secure with a toothpick. Place in an 8 inch greased baking dish. Combine water, oil and the rest of the soup. Pour over chicken.

Bake at 375 degrees for 25-30 minutes, until juices run clear. Cook pasta according to the directions on the package. Place pasta onto small casserole dishes. Top pasta with a piece of chicken. Pour spaghetti sauce on chicken, sprinkle with cheese and bake 5 more minutes.

Spinach and Strawberry Salad

2 Tbsp. sesame seeds
1 Tbsp. poppy seeds
1/2 cup white sugar
1/2 cup olive oil
1/4 cup distilled white vinegar
1/4 tsp. paprika
1/4 tsp. Worcestershire sauce
1 Tbsp. minced onion
10 oz. fresh spinach - rinsed, dried and torn into
        bite-sized pieces
1 quart strawberries - cleaned, hulled and sliced
1/4 cup almonds, blanched and slivered

In a medium bowl, whisk together the sesame seeds, poppy seeds, sugar, olive oil, vinegar, paprika, Worcestershire sauce and onion. Cover, and chill for one hour.

In a large bowl, combine the spinach, strawberries and almonds. Pour dressing over salad and toss.

Refrigerate for 10 to 15 minutes before serving.

Aunt Donnie's Cherry Dessert

2 (21 oz.) cans cherry pie filling
     (You could also use apple or peach.)
1/2 cup sugar
1 (7 oz.) box apple cinnamon Jiffy Mix
1/2 tube of Ritz crackers (butter crackers), crushed
1 stick plus 2 Tbsp. butter, melted

Mix the pie filling, sugar and 2 Tbsp. of butter. Place in a greased 9x9 pan. Mix crackers and jiffy mix. Sprinkle over pie filling. Pour the rest of the butter over everything.

Bake at 375 degrees for 40 minutes or until brown. You can easily double it and bake in 9x13 pan.

St. Patrick's Day

> **Beef Brisket or**
> **Corned Beef**
> **Rice**
> **Cold Pea Salad**
> **Hope's Lime Salad**
> **Brownies**
> Topped with green mint frosting

Cold Pea Salad

1 (10 oz.) pkg. frozen peas, thawed
1 cup celery, chopped
1 cup cauliflower, chopped
4 slices bacon, fried and crumbled (You could use
        cubes of ham in place of bacon.)
1 Tbsp. Dijon mustard
1/2 cup nuts, chopped
1/2 cup sour cream
1/2 cup ranch dressing
1/2 cup green onion, chopped
1 clove garlic, pressed

Toss together and serve cold on lettuce.

Glorified Garlic Bread

3/4 cup butter or margarine, softened
1/2 cup mayonnaise
3 cups (12 oz.) cheddar cheese, grated
1/2 cup Parmesan cheese, grated
2 green onions, chopped
1 tsp. Italian seasoning
1 garlic clove, minced
1 loaf French bread

Beat butter and mayonnaise together. Then add the rest of the ingredients except the bread. Slice the bread in two lengthwise and spread with the butter and mayonnaise mixture.

Broil 3-5 minutes until brown and bubbly.

Tip

When making rice on St. Patrick's Day, add a few drops of green food coloring to the water before tossing in the rice.

Hope's Lime Salad

Here's a recipe that just screams St. Patty's Day. Not only is it green, but it uses all that cabbage you got on sale the week of St. Patrick's Day. The ingredients are different but it makes a very light and refreshing salad when served on a lettuce leaf.

2 (3 oz.) pkgs. of lime gelatin
1 cup boiling water
1 (13 oz.) can evaporated milk
3/4 cup mayonnaise
1 (20 oz.) can crushed pineapple
2 cups cabbage, finely chopped
1 cup nuts, chopped

Dissolve gelatin in boiling water. Add milk. Fold in mayonnaise. Add the rest of the ingredients and pour into a 9x13 pan. Chill.

Easter

Spiced Honey Ham
Boiled New Red Potatoes
Deviled Eggs
Carrot and Celery Sticks
(in honor of the Easter Bunny of
course)
Peas and Pearl Onions
Pineapple Sour Cream Pie

Spiced Honey Ham

1/2 cup mustard
1/2 cup brown sugar
1/4 cup honey
1/4 cup orange juice
1 tsp. cloves
1 ham

Mix first 5 ingredients and pour over ham. Cook ham according to directions on the package, basting every 30 minutes.

Pineapple Sour Cream Pie

This dessert is a great change from all the sweets everyone has probably had from the Easter Bunny on Easter morning.

1 (5 1/2 oz.) pkg. instant vanilla pudding
1 (8 oz.) can crushed pineapple (plus juice)
2 cups sour cream
1 Tbsp. sugar
1 baked pie crust
whipped topping

Combine everything but the crust and the whipped topping and beat slowly for 1 minute. Pour into the crust and chill 3 hours. When ready to serve, top with whipped topping.

4th of July

Stuffed Bacon Cheeseburgers
Grilled Veggie Medley
Potato Salad
Watermelon and Cantaloupe Cubes
Cranberry Lemonade
Tony the Tiger Bites

Stuffed Bacon Cheeseburgers

1 lb. ground beef
3 Tbsp. ranch dressing
4 slices bacon, cooked and crumbled
2 slices American cheese, quartered (It's the 4th of
     July -- You must use American! :-)

Mix 2 tablespoons of dressing with ground beef and
flatten into 8 thin patties. Mix the rest of the dressing
with bacon and spoon about a tablespoon onto 4
patties.

Lay 2 quarters of the cheese on top of the bacon mix.
Then top with the other 4 patties. Pinch the edges of
the patties together, sealing well.

Grill 7-9 minutes on each side until done. Serve on a
bun with tomato, lettuce, or a French fried onion ring
(the kind that come in a can). Serves 4.

Grilled Veggie Medley

1/2 cup butter
1/4 cup Italian dressing
3 ears corn on the cob, cut into 2 inch pieces
2-3 red, green, or yellow peppers, cut into 1 inch
       pieces
1 zucchini, cut into 1/4 inch slices
10 large mushrooms

Toss all veggies in butter and dressing. Place in a covered, disposable pan and grill for 5 minutes or cook on medium high heat. Stir and grill for 5 more minutes until veggies are tender.

You can mix and match the kinds of veggies you use. For example, if you have no zucchini, you can substitute another piece of corn or add one or two peppers.

Cranberry Lemonade

Add 1/4 to 1/2 cup cranberry juice to a quart of your favorite lemonade.

Tony the Tiger Bites

These are as easy as Rice Krispy treats, but with a different twist.

1 (10 oz.) pkg. marshmallows
1/4 cup margarine
1/3 cup peanut butter
7 1/2 cups frosted flakes cereal

In a 4 quart microwave mixing bowl, melt marshmallows and margarine for 3 minutes on high, stirring after 1 1/2 minutes. Blend in peanut butter. Add cereal. Mix quickly. Press into a 9x13 greased pan. Cut into squares.

Halloween

Chili
Cornbread
Vegetable Tray
Mulled Apple Cider
Caramel Apples

Chili

1/2 lb. each hamburger and ground sausage
1 can (48 oz.) tomato juice
1 tsp. onion powder
1 tsp. garlic powder
1/2 tsp. sugar
2-3 Tbsp. chili powder, to taste
Salt and pepper to taste

Cook hamburger in a dutch oven or large saucepan. Drain. Add the rest of the ingredients. Simmer for 4-8 hours. Serve with grated cheese on top. You could put this in a crockpot and cook on low for 8 hours.

Add ins: You can add in things like a can of kidney beans, onion or canned tomatoes.

Caramel Apples

1 (14 oz.) bag of caramels (about 2 cups)
2 Tbsp. milk
5-6 apples

Place a piece of wax paper on a tray. Sprinkle the wax paper with powdered sugar or butter it. Wash apples. Remove stems, stick wooden (Popsicle) sticks in the opposite ends from the stems. Place milk and unwrapped caramels in a large measuring cup. Microwave about 2 minutes until melted.

Place on a tray or roll in:

Crushed Oreo, chocolate chip, grahams or other cookies
Chocolate or white chocolate chips
Candy corns
Sprinkles
Nuts
M & M's

Tip

For better dipping, place apples in the fridge overnight before dipping or in the freezer while you are melting the caramels.

If you don't have sticks, use a sturdy plastic fork. These are sometimes easier for the kids to handle.

Thanksgiving

Turkey/with Stuffing
Mashed Potatoes
Relish Dish
Sweet Potatoes
Green Bean Casserole
Cranberry Sauce
Dinner Rolls
Pecan, Pumpkin, Apple Pie

Many of you are wondering how Thanksgiving can be quick and easy? Actually, it can be one of the easiest meals to make. First of all, you don't have to stew over what the menu is going to be. You usually expect to have turkey for the meat, mashed potatoes, stuffing, green bean casserole, cranberry sauce, dinner rolls, pecan, pumpkin and apple pie. See-- the menu is a no-brainer. Now I know some of you will add your own favorite dishes but this is the basic menu to start with.

Another thing that makes Thanksgiving so easy is that the dishes themselves are very easy to make. Just put the turkey into the pan, cover and bake. For stuffing, use a box mix. Peel potatoes and then cook and mash them. Open a can of cranberry sauce, slice it and serve. Buy some dinner rolls and warm.

Lastly, we worry over Thanksgiving because we often have to feed a bigger crowd than we are used to feeding and often they are people we are worried about impressing, but take a deep breath and relax. One thing about feeding more people is that they will usually offer to bring part of the meal, which can be a great help.

Moneywise, Thanksgiving is a very frugal meal. Turkey, green beans and potatoes are all normally very inexpensive foods but, at Thanksgiving, they all go on sale for almost nothing. Stock up. There is nothing to say you can't eat cranberry sauce in March or sweet potatoes in February. Also, even though we have given you a long menu, you can pick and choose. You don't have to make everything on the menu. Just do what you need and can afford.

For some of the recipes below I will give you a longer or "from scratch" version and a quick version.

Tip

If you expect a large crowd, save time peeling by using half fresh potatoes and half instant. Say you are having 20 people over. Peel 10 potatoes, cook and mash them. Then mix the same amount of instant potatoes (made according to the package instructions) in with the fresh potatoes.

Roast Turkey

1 turkey, 20-22 lbs.
1 stick margarine or butter

Defrost frozen turkey for several days in the
refrigerator according to the directions on the
package. Line a roasting pan with aluminum foil.
Remove the insides of the turkey and save for giblet
gravy or for fried livers and gizzards.

Lay turkey, **breast side down**, in the pan and place
the stick of butter on the inside. Cover tightly with
aluminum foil. Bake at 250 degrees for 1 hour.
Reduce heat to 200 degrees and roast for 10-15
hours. Cooking time can be longer to fit your
schedule. Test with a meat thermometer to make sure
the temperature in the thigh is 180 degrees.

If I have a 20-22 lb. turkey, I put it in the oven one
hour before I go to bed. (That way I can turn it down
to 200 degrees and sometimes I turn it down to 180
degrees before I go to bed.) It will be done by noon
the next day. Because it is cooking at such a low
temperature, if you aren't going to eat until 1-2 PM, it
will stay just fine in the oven until then.

If I have a 10 lb. turkey, I put it in the oven early on
Thanksgiving morning (about 6 or 7 AM in order to eat
at noon. You don't need to worry too much about it
getting done. An hour or two before the meal, check it
and see how it is doing. If it isn't cooking quickly
enough, you can always raise the temperature to 350
degrees. With a 10 -12 lb. turkey, you only need to

use half of a stick (about 4 Tbsp.) of butter. You can place it in a large crockpot on low, too.

This is the best turkey you will ever eat. The meat will just fall off the bones so you will have to serve it already carved. It will be very juicy and moist.

Turkey Gravy

3-4 cups turkey juices/drippings
1/4 cup flour
salt and pepper to taste

Pour turkey juices/drippings into a sauce pan. Whisk in flour. Add salt and pepper. Simmer for about 15 minutes, stirring once in a while until it is the right consistency.

If the gravy is too strong or you need to stretch it a little, you can add a small amount of water. Another way I used to do it (either way works) is to dissolve the flour in 1/2 cup of cold water and then whisk it into the turkey juices.

Crunchy Green Bean Casserole

4 slices bacon, cooked and crumbled
1 (10.75 oz.) can cream of mushroom soup
1 (8 oz.) can water chestnuts, drained and chopped
3/4 cup milk
2 (15 oz.) cans green beans, drained
ground black pepper to taste
1 1/3 cups French-fried onions

Preheat oven to 350 degrees. In a 1 1/2 quart casserole dish, mix together the bacon, soup, water chestnuts, milk, green beans and a pinch of black pepper.

Bake for 30 minutes or until heated through.
Stir and top with French fried onions. Bake for 5 additional minutes or until onions are golden brown.

Add-ins: You could add mushrooms to this recipe, replace French fried onions with cheddar cheese and stir in a spoonful or two of the bacon grease with the green beans just to add that much more flavor.

Quick Version: Warm some green beans and canned bacon bits in the microwave and then sprinkle with crumbled French fried onions before serving.

Grandma Tatum's Stuffing

8-10 cups dried bread, cubed or torn (You can use
      anything, including hot dog buns, dinner rolls or
      French bread.)
1/2-1 lb. pork sausage
1/2-1 onion (or onion powder to taste)
3 eggs, slightly beaten
1 1/2 cups broth*
1 chicken bouillon cube
1/4-1/2 cup margarine
3 heaping tsp. ground sage
1 small bag or box of seasoned croutons
salt and pepper

Cube and tear bread in a very large mixing bowl and
let set out overnight to dry.

Fry sausage and onion. I don't like celery in my
dressing but if you do you can add it at this time.
Drain sausage and onion and add it to the bowl of
bread.

Pour broth into a large measuring cup. Add margarine
and bouillon cube and heat in the microwave to melt
margarine and bouillon cubes. Pour this mixture and
eggs over bread. Add sage, salt, pepper (and onion
powder if not using onions) and croutons.

Using your hands, mush it all together until well
mixed. Place in a well greased casserole dish or pan.
Cover. Bake at 350 degrees for 30-45 minutes.

If you like your stuffing soft on the inside with a crispy
crust, just remove the cover for the last 15 minutes. If

your dressing seems too dry, add a little milk for more moisture.

*For broth, I simmer the turkey neck and giblets in a pan of water for an hour or two as soon as I take them out of the turkey. Then I use this water and some broth from my turkey, which has been cooking, to make my 1 1/2 cups.

Quick Version: Use a box of stuffing and use some of your turkey broth for the liquid. You can also add some cooked ground sausage, mushrooms, celery, apples or giblets if you like.

Tip

You can adjust any of these stuffing ingredients to suit your taste and, if you want, you can add different things to the dish.

For example, you can replace some of the bread with cornbread or you can add mushrooms, celery, apples, giblets and many other things according to your own taste. This is one of those recipes that looks complicated but is really easy once you make it.

Pumpkin Pie

2 eggs
1 (15 oz.) can pumpkin
3/4 cup sugar
1/2 tsp. salt
1 tsp. cinnamon
1/2 tsp. ground ginger
1/4 tsp. ground cloves
1 (12 oz.) can evaporated milk
1 pie crust

Blend all ingredients except the pie crust together in a bowl. Bake the pie crust at 350 degrees for 1-2 minutes until crust starts to puff with small bubbles. Watch carefully. Then remove it from the oven.

Pour everything into the pie crust and bake at 425 degrees for 15 minutes. Then turn the oven down to 350 degrees for 45 minutes. When a knife is inserted into the center of the pie and comes out clean, it is done. Makes one pie.

Pecan Pie

1 stick butter
1 cup light corn syrup
1 cup sugar
3 large eggs
1/2 tsp. lemon juice
1 tsp. vanilla
dash of salt
1 1/4 cups pecans, chopped
1 (8-9 inch) unbaked pie crust

Brown butter in a pan until golden brown. Do not burn.
Cool.

Combine other ingredients in the order given in a
separate bowl. Mix well. Blend in cooled butter well.
Pour into pie crust.

Bake 10 minutes at 425 degrees and then 40 minutes
at 325 degrees. Makes one pie.

Tip

When using pecans or any nuts, roast them in the
microwave or the oven to bring out their flavor before
you use them.

Christmas

Best Baked Ham
Mashed Potatoes
Candied Sweet Potatoes
Broccoli and Cauliflower Salad
Red Salad
Crescent Rolls
Pecan, Pumpkin or Cherry Pie
Christmas Cookies and Candy

Best Baked Ham

10 pounds pre-cooked ham
1/2 can (6 oz.) cola-flavored carbonated beverage
1 cup brown sugar
1/2 tsp. cloves

Remove any excess fat from ham. Place the ham in a large roasting pan or roasting bag and place in a baking dish.

Pour cola over ham. If using a roasting bag, remove as much air as possible or seal with foil. Let it sit overnight in the fridge. Before baking, mix the brown sugar and cloves and rub on the ham.

Prick a few holes in the roasting bag (if you're using one) to let steam escape and bake at 275 degrees for 4 to 5 hours. Let rest 15 minutes. Pour off excess juice and slice.

Broccoli and Cauliflower Salad

4 cups broccoli, cut in pieces
4 cups cauliflower, cut in pieces
2 cups celery, sliced
1/2 cup green olives, sliced
1 avocado, cut into small cubes
1/4 to 1/2 cup sunflower seeds
Italian dressing

Put everything into a bowl and sprinkle with Italian dressing (to taste). You can have everything cut and ready the day before except the avocado and dressing.

Tip

Put regular or sweet potatoes in the crockpot to cook to make things quicker and easier and to free up space in the oven.

Delicious Red Jello Salad

1/2 cup boiling water
1 small package cherry Jello
1/4 to 1/2 cup red hot candies
1 1/2 cups applesauce

Dissolve Jello and candies in boiling water. I usually do this in a small saucepan so I can keep it on low heat to warm while dissolving the candies. When the candies are mostly dissolved, add the applesauce and chill until set.

This salad is a family favorite and a staple for Christmas! The family says that we can't celebrate Christmas without the Red Jello Salad! ;-) It adds a beautiful red color to the Christmas table and children and men seem to really love it.

Tip

I like to keep Christmas dinner as simple and easy as possible. Here are some ways to keep it simple:

- In place of candied sweet potatoes you could have baked sweet potatoes. Just wrap them and place them in the oven with the ham.

- You don't need to spend all Christmas morning making homemade rolls. Buy a couple of cans of crescents. They usually are on sale at this time.

My Menus

Monday

_____

_____

_____

Tuesday

_____

_____

_____

Wednesday

_____

_____

_____

Thursday

_____

_____

_____

Friday

_____

_____

_____

Saturday

_____

_____

_____

Sunday

_____

_____

_____

Index

Biscuits, Poppy's, 92
Blue Cheese Hamburgers, 22
Boston Cream Pie Cupcakes, 37
Breads
  Apple Yogurt Muffins, 122
  Biscuits, Poppy's, 92
  Cinnamon Roll Pudding, 18
  Glorified Garlic Bread, 143
Broccoli and Cauliflower Salad, 162
Brownie Cake, 93
Butterscotch Pudding Parfaits, 43

C
Candy Bar Truffle, 118
Cauliflower/Olive Salad, 103
Cakes
  Angel Food Delight, 95
  Banana Cake, 89
  Boston Cream Pie Cupcakes, 37
  Brownie Cake, 93
  Marbled Strawberry Cake, 39
  Mint Brownie Cake, 98
Caramel Apples, 151
Cherry Dessert, Barb's, 71
Cheese Egg, 129
Cheesy Rice with Peas, 87
Chili, 150
Cherry Delight, 80
Cherry Dessert, Aunt Donnie's 141
Cherry Marshmallow Dessert, 105

Chicken
  Chicken Croissants, 88
  Chicken Marinara, 139
  Chicken Nuggets, 87
  Chicken Pitas, 81
  Chicken Salad Sandwiches, 83

Fruit Dip, 116
Fruit Salad, 63
Fruit Slush Cups, 102
Instant Peach Cobbler, 50
Orange Creme Dessert, 107
Orange Salad, 30
Raspberry Rhapsody Salad, 58
Royal Fruit Cup, 94
Spinach/Strawberry Salad, 140
Strawberry Dessert, 61
Fruit Cup, 28
Fruit Dip, 116
Fruit Salad, 63
Fruit Slush Cups, 102

G
Garlic Broccoli, 52
Garlic Green Beans, 20
German Baked Beans, 59
Glorified Garlic Bread, 143
Grandma Tatum's Stuffing, 157
Grandma's Banana Dessert, 41
Green and Gold Salad, 32
Green Beans, 69
Grilled Apple Swiss Cheese Sandwich, 126
Grilled Veggie Medley, 148

H
Hasty Hamburger and Beans, 24
Hoagie Sandwiches, 120
Hope's Lime Salad, 144
Hot Ham and Cheese Sandwiches, 67
Hot Jam Sandwiches, 128

J
Joe Froggers Cookies, 33
Juicy Roasted Chicken, 96

K
Ketchicola Roast, 19

L
Lemon Fluff, 76

M
Marbled Strawberry Cake, 39
Marinated Pork Chops, 62
Marshmallow Bars, 70
Mexican Chef Salad, 119
Mexican Spaghetti, 38
Mexican Summer Squash, 75
Mint Brownie Cake, 98
Mystery Meatballs, 32

N
No Bake Peanut Butter Cookies, 90
No Mess Dinner, 55
Nutty Ham Pitas, 53

O
One Dish Vegetarian Meal, 121
Orange Creme Dessert, 107
Orange Floats, 65
Orange Salad, 30

P
Parmesan Baked Fish, 108
Peach cobbler, Instant, 50
Peanut Butter Cream Pie, 125
Pecan Fish, 110
Pecan Pie, 160
Picante Chicken, 90
Pineapple Sour Cream Pie, 146
Pinwheel Pizza Loaf, 36
Pizza Bake, 44
Pizzas, Mini Breakfast, 134

Order Form

Please send me:

____copies of **Dining On A Dime**   @ $21.95 ea $_____

____copies of **Menus From Dining on a Dime**

@ $7.95 ea $_____

____copies of **Dig Out Of Debt**   @ $17.95 ea $_____

____copies of **Penny Pinching Mama** @$12.95 ea$_____

____copies of **Quick And Easy Menus on a Dime**

@ $14.95 ea $_____

* *Shipping & Handling* (**US only**) 1 book $4.50 $_____

Each Additional Book $1.00 $_____

Sub Total $_____

Colorado Residents add 4.9% sales tax $_____

TOTAL $_____

* Canadian Orders Triple Postage

Please enclose check payable to *Living on A Dime.*

Ship to:

Name_____

Address_____ Apt #_____

City_____ State _____Zip _____

E-Mail _____ Phone_____

E-Books or credit card orders may be placed online at :
www.LivingOnADime.com

<u>**Mail to:**</u>

Living On A Dime
P.O. Box 193
Mead, CO 80542